SW
B   Spence

Pioneer Women of Abilene

DATE DUE

NOV 7 84			

Imperial Public Library
Imperial, Texas

Pioneer Women

Of Abilene

By

Vernon Gladden Spence

Introduction
By
Katharyn Duff

Drawings
By
Julia Matthews Wilkinson

EAKIN PRESS   ★   BURNET, TEXAS

Imperial Public Library
Imperial, Texas

FIRST EDITION

Copyright © 1981

By Vernon Gladden Spence

Published in the United States of America
By Eakin Press, P.O. Drawer AG, Burnet, Texas 78611

ALL RIGHTS RESERVED

ISBN 0-89015-281-0

For Wanda

Other books by the author: *Colonel Morgan Jones: Grand Old Man of Texas Railroading*, 1971 and *Judge Legett of Abilene: A Texas Frontier Profile*, 1977.

"Standing Guard" Over the Family Jewels

PREFACE

Until recent years, historians assumed that the role of women in history did not deserve serious inquiry. Since women were not a part of the power structure in the United States, scholars believed that there was nothing of consequence to say about them. They mentioned that women participated in reform movements (temperance was usually a convenient example), and they wrote that women and small children were exploited in factories. Most other recognition was limited to a few modest comments on such female personalities as the Grimke sisters, Harriet Beecher Stowe, Jane Addams, Susan B. Anthony, Elizabeth Cady Stanton, and Carrie Nation.

Having recognized these familiar names, the way was clear for men to write about men. History therefore was a study of man's activities on the battlefield, in the pulpit, in the business office, and in political office. Women were not equal partners in building America; hence, it was assumed there was no place for them in the annals of history.

When women later embarked upon a major campaign for woman suffrage, they won for themselves a few additional paragraphs in the history books. Recognition was slow, however, and scholars who mentioned suffragists' activities almost invariably disparaged women by calling them "suffragettes."

A dramatic turn from this boorish attitude is now underway. Acceptance of woman's place in United States history is evident in almost all serious studies. Many younger historians who are leading the way are women—and that should surprise no one. A few of them suggest that this new field should be left entirely to women historians, although most recognize that there is more than enough to be done on the subject to keep both sexes busy. Obviously I agree with the majority, for I have focused this study upon three pioneer women of West Texas.

The current popularity of reevaluating women's roles in frontier history is especially evident. Here, too, women historians are in the lead, although such male historians as T.A.

Larsen and Robert E. Riegel have long been writing about the frontierswoman. These and other scholars helped to kindle my own interest in the subject, but my major incentive came during the '70s while I researched *Judge Legett of Abilene: A Texas Frontier Profile*. The women in Legett's life convinced me of the need to write this book.

Judge Legett was a typical Horatio Alger rags-to-riches hero. More than that, he was "an epitome of his section of Texas" as historian Rupert Norval Richardson has written. But Legett was by no means entirely self-made. Sophia Wyers Bryan, Legett's mother-in-law; Lora Bryan Legett, his wife; and Ruth Legett Jones, his daughter, contributed importantly to his success. It is true that Legett proved his potential before any of them entered his life, but his success was greater, his accomplishments more impressive, and his contributions to his community more significant because of their influence upon him. Publication restrictions concerning the Legett biography forced a major reduction in the length of the original manuscript, and the consequent deletions included many of their contributions to Legett's success. In a sense, therefore, this book is an effort to set the record straight—to give credit where credit is overdue.

Sophia Wyers Bryan, Lora Bryan Legett, and Ruth Legett Jones represent three generations of a family whose westwardly moving ancestors migrated through Pennsylvania, Virginia, North Carolina, Tennessee, Alabama, Mississippi, Arkansas, and Texas. Their experiences were typical of the tens of thousands of other pioneering families who moved west. All of them, of course, shared a common conviction: they were manifestly destined to find their fortunes "just a little farther west."

They remained typical of the masses of pioneers for generation after generation until Sophia Wyers Bryan (representing the family's first Texas generation) and Washington Carroll Bryan combined their energies and talents and developed a remarkably successful cattle and cutting-horse ranch in Falls County, Texas. Because the degree of their success far exceeded the average, the Bryans were no longer typical. Nevertheless, their westward migration shifted into another pattern which was in turn typical of other affluent pioneers: They sold their limited acres in Falls County and moved to the wide open spaces of West Texas.

The Bryans' three children, who were the family's second Texas generation, and who are represented in this book by Lora Bryan Legett, also fell into a pattern typical of the more economically successful pioneers: They migrated westward no more. Instead, Lora Legett and her husband, K.K. Legett, heirs to one-third of her parents' 23,000 acres in Taylor, Jones, Fisher, and Stonewall counties, sank deep family roots into West Texas soil. Through ranching, farming, and the legal profession, they expanded their inherited fortune through their own efforts. Their prominent position in Abilene's business and social circles passed in turn to the Legetts' three children, the third Texas generation, who are represented in this book by Ruth Legett Jones. With her husband, Percy Jones, a civil engineer and railroad builder, she accumulated through inheritance and the expansion of their farm, ranch, railroad, and oil properties, one of the largest fortunes in Texas. As a consequence, Ruth Legett Jones eventually became one of the most generous philanthropists in the state.

Thus, while the Bryan-Legett-Jones patterns of westward migration followed several typical patterns, the degree of their economic success was manifestly untypical. Largely because of this affluence, therefore, the life stories of Sophia, Lora, and Ruth are also untypical of stereotyped frontierswomen. Among other obvious advantages, they were less worn by heavy work in house and field and less isolated from their neighbors. Perhaps they were readily accepted as equals by virtually all male members of their families. There is no hint in any of the records I have seen that their husbands held to the dogma that women's minds and talents are inferior. That is to say, they did not fit into another well-known female stereotype as bejewelled status symbols of their husbands' affluence. They were, instead, a part of that success.

These frontierswomen had even less in common with the more familiar stereotypes created by the overactive imaginations of earlier writers. They were not, for example, typical of the Calamity Janes who generally acted more like men than women; they were not "saints in sunbonnets"; they were not suffragists, or temperance reformers bent on ridding the frontier of drunkards; and they were not "ladies of the night" with hearts of gold. Even less were they representatives of Emerson Hough's "gaunt and sad-faced woman, face hidden in a ragged sunbonnet, sitting on the front seat of a wagon, following her lord wherever he might lead." Probably at no time in their lives were they saddled with the "utter loneliness" that haunted Everett Dick's frontierswomen. Instead, they were much nearer the image of Richard A. Bartlett's pioneer woman in *The New Country:* "She held her head high, and her bright eyes searched the horizon for what lay ahead. She shared with her husband a faith in their future. She was a builder, along with her husband; she knew her value."

It would be more to the point to record that Sophia Wyers Bryan, Lora Bryan Legett, and Ruth Legett Jones were not typical of *any* stereotyped woman, and I would suggest that historians should abandon what appears to be a continued tendency to categorize female types in history. Writers in general should concentrate, instead, on some of the more obvious points made by historian Glenda Riley and others who claim that women were on the frontier in far greater numbers than earlier historians have been led to believe; that their types were as varied as those of the men they married; and that their accomplishments—although less public—are nevertheless worthy of note. If this book fails to demonstrate this point, the problem lies with the author, not with his subjects.

I do not mean to imply, however, that I alone am responsible for piecing together their stories. The reader should have no trouble, for example, in recognizing my indebtedness to the late Ruth Legett Jones. Innumerable interviews [she insisted upon calling them conversations] revealed her sensitivity to the problems of the historian. Her love of history caused her to look upon all historians as friends and colleagues, and the few who held themselves aloof at history conventions only convinced her that *she* had said or done something to displease them.

Rupert Norval Richardson, distinguished Professor of History at Hardin-Simmons University (Mrs. Jones's long-time favorite historian and my favorite mentor), has assisted me through the years in innumerable ways. This project has been no exception. Constantly on the move, Professor Richardson never fails to stop and lend assistance whenever he is called upon.

Katharyn Duff, newspaperwoman and author, is the perfect personification of the adage that reminds us all to seek out a busy person when we need a helping hand. Immersed in her own writing projects, she readily agreed to write the introduction to this book. Beth Duff, who can spot a misspelled word from thirty paces, further increased my indebtedness to the Duff household.

Maude King, retired professor of English at Hardin-Simmons University, proved to me once again that she is the best writing consultant and proofreader in the business. Only my former mentor, Vernie E. Newman, professor emeritus of history at McMurry College, who is no longer able to assist me, could challenge Professor King's genius in turning my writing efforts into readable English.

Also in the Abilene area, I am indebted to the following friends for a variety of aids and encouragements: Professors Paul Lack, Lynn Lack, and Henry Doscher at McMurry College; Melvin Holt and Eugene Allen, members of the Dodge-Jones Foundation staff; Nena Kate Lewis, William Lewis, Texas Wagstaff, and Ruth Williamson, who provided new insights into the delightful personality of their friend Ruth Jones; especially to Julia Jones Matthews, who is the daughter, granddaughter, and great-granddaughter of the three subjects of this book.

At George Mason University, I am indebted to Charlene Calder, Betty Lockhart, and Joan Atkins, who were always on hand to assist in my endless cries for secretarial help; and to the staff at the University Word Processing Center under the direction of Curtis Mackereth.

At home I am indebted to Forrest M. Davis, Jr. and Rebecca Gladden Davis who convinced me that Virginians like to read about Texans; to Kirk McKinnon, Bobbie Hull McKinnon, and Hattie Kathryn Childress, who convinced me that some Texans will read a book by a Virginian about Texas; to my mother, Ruth Gladden Spence, and to my deceased father, Vernon Lewis Spence, who always seemed eager to read anything I ever wrote; and to my children John Randolph, Deborah Anne, and Kevin Douglas, who grew from childhood to maturity wondering if books were written only about Bryans, Legetts, and Joneses.

And finally I am indebted to my wife, Wanda Smith Spence, who suffers with me through every page I write, and who manages to convince me that each little effort is worthwhile.

George Mason University   Vernon Gladden Spence
                                                   May 2, 1980

West Texas Courting: 1915 Style.

CONTENTS

Preface v

Introduction xiii

Part One: Sophia Wyers Bryan (1837-1904) 3

    Author's Foreword to Conversations with Ruth Legett Jones 8

    Conversations with Ruth Legett Jones 10

Part Two: Lora Bryan Legett (1867-1923) 27

    Conversations with Ruth Legett Jones 32

Part Three: Ruth Legett Jones (1892-1978) 63

    Conversations with Ruth Legett Jones 70

Epilogue 111

Bibliographical Note 112

"In the Sweeeeeet Bye and Bye . . ."

INTRODUCTION

Ruth Legett Jones and Vernon Gladden Spence became acquainted in 1966 when she agreed to open for his examination family papers and documents so that he could research the life of Colonel Morgan Jones. Colonel Jones, one of America's most successful railroad builders, was a man of mystery little known in history because, during his lifetime, he avoided all forms of publicity. Known to the family as "the Old Mahn," he was the bachelor-uncle of Ruth Jones's late husband Percy. Her agreement to open the Old Mahn's records after all these years came at a moment in 1967 when Spence, an instructor at McMurry College in Abilene, had completed class work for his doctorate at the University of Colorado. He needed a dissertation subject which the University would approve. Here, at last, was exactly what he needed. Thanks to Ruth Jones, Spence had access to information which would please any historian.

So the two became acquainted, and it was respect at first glance. The respect grew to become devotion. For Ruth Jones, here was an able historian to whom she could release highly personal papers so that through them he could preserve a piece of history which had long been cloaked. For Spence, here was a delightful, helpful, witty woman who made it possible for him to do basic research. He did his job well. He was granted his doctorate. His dissertation was published by the University of Oklahoma Press.

The Jones biography brought career changes to the Spence family. Spence, a native of Tangier Island in the Chesapeake Bay, accepted in 1970 a position with George Mason University, the State University in Northern Virginia, at Fairfax. The change did not, however, disturb the Jones-Spence relationship. While researching the Morgan Jones story, Spence had become interested in the story of Ruth Jones's father, K.K. Legett, and was hard at work on this second biography when he moved to Virginia. The Legett book, *Judge Legett of Abilene,* was published by the Texas A&M University Press in November 1977.

And then there was another book which Spence had in mind. His intimate study of the family had brought him to a new fascination, the story of three pioneer women: Sophia Wyers Bryan, her daughter Lora Bryan Legett, and her granddaughter Ruth Legett Jones. The three were by no means typical frontierswomen. All three were unusually interested in cultural affairs, unusually influential. Spence set himself to researching the three through his "conversations" with Jones. As Spence writes in his bibliographical essay, "For twelve years we talked . . . and talked," sometimes over the telephone between Texas and Virginia, at other times at her Abilene office. Then their talks came to a sudden halt.

Ruth Legett Jones died unexpectedly at her Abilene home on October 14, 1978.

What, then, should Spence do with all his data he had collected during his long, but yet uncompleted, conversations with Ruth Jones? The two so trusted each other that she had related to him thoughts, impressions, even events never before shared with others. Spence did with his material what those who knew Jones will consider proper. He combined his findings into *Pioneer Women of Abilene: A Trilogy,* using an unusual format, a "question and answer" presentation of their talks.

The book gives rare insight into the complex characteristics which made Ruth Legett Jones an extraordinary person, a discerning, compassionate, shy, private gentlewoman who kept her heartbreaks to herself. She was remarkably intelligent, with an innate wisdom which guided her through a changing world. She was sensitive to others' needs, and her sense of humor was delightful. She raised the criterion for her town and for her fellow townsmen, which was no ordinary accomplishment.

Abilene, Texas   Katharyn Duff
June 12, 1980

PART ONE

Abandoning Ship When Chains Rattle

SOPHIA WYERS BRYAN (1837-1904)

SOPHIA WYERS BRYAN
(1837-1904)

Sophia Ann Wyers was born January 15, 1837, on a farm near an abandoned Indian village in the Republic of Texas. She was the second of fourteen children born to Robert Wyers and Harriet Ship Wyers between 1835 and 1863. Political upheavals at that time and place were so frequent that, although the Wyerses never moved from their original farm, their first child was born a citizen of Mexico, their next six children (including Sophia) were born citizens of the Republic of Texas, and their seven youngest were born citizens of the United States.

Sophia's parents had moved to the frontier and cleared land for farming in a manner not unlike earlier generations of Wyerses. It was traditional in that sense, therefore, that they looked to the West to seek their fortunes as farmers.

The first of their American ancestors—who spelled their surname Weyers—settled in Pennsylvania. From there they moved to Augusta County, Virginia, founded a village, and named it Weyers Cave. Later Weyer's descendants moved to Alabama and thence to the east Texas frontier. For reasons unknown, the Weyerses who settled in Texas changed the spelling of their name to Wyers.

By the time that Sophia was twelve years old, a sufficient number of other pioneering families had settled in the area to permit the organization of McLennan County. The old Indian village near them, then occupied by Anglo settlers, was named Waco to honor the tribe of Indians who first settled there.

There is no evidence that Sophia received formal education beyond reading, writing, and arithmetic. The common belief at that time, however—that coeducation was morally wrong—does not account for Sophia's limited education. Records show that her grandfather helped to establish Waco Female College in McLennan County, Texas. Primitive frontier conditions during Sophia's childhood, therefore, is a more likely explanation for her lack of formal education. On the other hand, she was the second eldest of fourteen children and so it is possible that her mother needed Sophia at home to help with domestic chores.

Harriet Wyers's youngest two children were not yet born when Sophia, her eldest daughter, married Washington Carroll Bryan on January 9, 1859. Following a custom common in that day, Sophia, thirteen years younger than her husband, never called him by any other name than "Mr. Bryan."

Bryan was a young man in his early twenties when in 1846 he left the family home in Williamson County, Tennessee, and sought employment in Panole County, Mississippi, as a blacksmith. From Mississippi he journeyed to Texas, settled first at Galveston, later at Port Lavaca, and still later at Gonzales. On May 5, 1851, he volunteered for six months' service with the Texas Rangers. By the time of his discharge on November 5, he had decided to establish a cattle and horse ranch on Keechi Creek near Marlin in Falls County. The ranch prospered from the beginning, and by the time of his marriage his T-Diamond brand cattle and fine cutting horses were known and admired throughout the state.

In late 1859 the Bryans' only son, John, was born. A daughter, Julia, was born in 1862 during the course of the Civil War, and in 1867 their second daughter and last child, Lora, was born.

Sophia managed both home and ranch while her husband served in the Confederate army. Upon the war's conclusion, Bryan, having attained the rank of Colonel, returned to his family and started anew raising cattle and horses. By the late 1870s the Bryans had prospered to the point that cattle and horses had overpopulated their Falls County acreage. Consequently, Colonel and Mrs. Bryan began to look for more ranch land farther west.

Scattered evidence suggests that Sophia was a major influence in her husband's continued success as a rancher. In many respects she was a conventional housewife and mother, but through the years she developed a strong ambition to "be somebody." From the beginning of her marriage she was almost completely absorbed in her husband's work, yet she never appeared to consider herself inferior to him and, in turn, he soon learned to value her judgment in business matters.

Sophia raised her son and two daughters with a calm but firm hand. She was an undemonstrative woman whose children in later years could recall few signs of affection. Nevertheless, they never felt deprived of love or attention. Perhaps her own childhood experiences contributed to her reserve. As a child Sophia tended her younger brothers and sisters, milked cows, tended gardens, fed chickens, cooked meals, and cleaned the house. Life was a constant struggle for survival on the outer edges of settlement and there was no time to spoil or pamper children.

As a young woman with children of her own, Sophia repeated those domestic chores—but only so long as it was absolutely necessary. Childraising, housecleaning, and cooking were not for her a new and exciting adventure. It would be a mistake, however, to look upon Sophia Bryan as a silent, brooding, emotionally frustrated woman longing for an easier life. She was, instead, an energetic, self-sufficient, and independent woman who was entirely able to care for herself, her children, and the T-Diamond ranch during her husband's absences.

Sophia was not the type, on the other hand, to concern herself with social reform or political causes. She was not interested in closing saloons, for example, or ridding the ranch of drunken cowboys; but when the necessity arose, she could shoot straight, cut cattle, and snap a snake's head with the flip of her wrist.

Generally uneducated herself, Sophia nevertheless inherited her male ancestors' interest in higher coeducation. She was pleased when her son John earned a bachelor's degree at The Agricultural and Mechanical College in Texas and a law degree from The Cumberland Law School in Tennessee, and she seemed equally proud when her younger daughter Lora attended Waco Female College in Texas and Wesleyan Female Institute in Virginia, both founded by her paternal ancestors.

Eventually, the Bryans located suitable ranch lands some

two hundred miles west in Taylor and Fisher counties. Both counties lay in the rolling plains area of central West Texas. Sophia showed no reluctance, even at middle age, to move (as her parents had done earlier) to another raw frontier settlement. She was not the type to cower from danger or risk, and certainly not typical of the "gaunt and sad-faced women" in Emerson Hough's western novels.

When Sophia Bryan moved to Abilene, a bustling, four-year-old cowtown along the Texas and Pacific railroad tracks in central Taylor County, she held her head high and looked only to the future. She would be somebody, and she instilled this attitude into her children.

Her son John and his bride Mattie Dashell, and her older daughter Julia, and her husband Sam Young, decided to move to Abilene with the elder Bryans. After a little persuasion, her younger daughter Lora agreed to delay her return to the Virginia school and accompany them to the West. When they arrived in Abilene they brought with them considerable wealth and a business reputation—at least among local ranchers. Eventually, Washington Carroll Bryan and his family accumulated 23,000 acres of land in Taylor, Fisher, Jones and Stonewall counties. The Bryans were not boastful nor pretentious people, however, and when in later years anyone asked Bryan how he managed to possess such a vast acreage he answered, with tongue-in-cheek, that he bought a buffalo dugout in Fisher County for $40 and, in appreciation for the payment, the owner threw in "all the land within a twenty-mile radius of the dugout."

Their arrival in Abilene attracted more than the usual newspaper attention. Much was written about their T-Diamond cattle and cutting-horses, and the editor seemed especially impressed by Bryan's military credentials as a former Texas Ranger and Confederate Army colonel. The editor also appreciated the "beauty and charm of Miss Lora" who, he informed the local Beau Brummels, was "completely unattached."

The Bryans' red-topped, two-story brick house on South First Street was large enough to justify Sophia to hire household help. Usually she had a cook and a cleaning woman to come in every day. She abhorred housework of any description, and she insisted that she was a poor cook. Her family never disputed the latter point. In later years, her grandchildren could never recall seeing Granny Bryan in her own kitchen. Having employed domestic help, Sophia left them alone and rarely praised or criticized their performance. She was far more interested in the activities of the male members of her family: her husband's ranching, her son's work as an attorney, or their negotiations for purchasing more land. She had, obviously, the instincts and interests of a businesswoman, but with little opportunity beyond the circle of her own family to develop them.

Sophia Wyers Bryan appeared to accept her station in life without complaint. She presided over her household and she served her husband as companion and consultant, but beyond that limited range she rarely ventured. It is not likely that her political or economic powerlessness outside her home bothered her: she was a Baptist, but there is no evidence that she was active in church work; she abhorred drunkards, but she never participated in temperance movements.

When in public view Sophia dressed well, with layers and layers of petticoats, but she did not concern herself with stylish dress. At middle age she could have afforded the usual status symbols of women—glittering jewels, velvet wraps, and even a pale complexion—but Sophia had no such interests.

Instead, Sophia's middle and later years were stamped by the memory of her childhood and her day-to-day struggle to help her family survive. As she matured she developed a driving ambition to succeed, to progress, to "be somebody," but an accumulation of wealth created no need for luxury. Not surprisingly, perhaps, she was more inclined to pamper her children. The narrow confines of Victorian morality never seemed to bother her one way or another, and she displayed a more enlightened attitude toward her children's social activities than most women of her era and region. She approved of, for instance, her younger daughter's wish to attend school in a distant state although Sophia had never traveled beyond the borders of Texas. At home, she never restricted her daughters' attendance at the opera house although many of Sophia's contemporaries frowned upon such entertainment for young women.

It was Sophia Wyers Bryan's fate to be a female version of Horatio Alger's success stories, and to die amidst considerable wealth. She could have managed with less. Dressed in linsey-woolsey, calico, and gingham during her childhood, Sophia was content in later life to wrap herself in flocks of petticoats, bone corsets, and velvet; she left it to her children and grandchildren to develop a taste for imported laces, grand pianos, and porcelain china.

FOREWORD TO CONVERSATIONS WITH RUTH LEGETT JONES

The following coversations between the author and Mrs. Jones were always informal and rarely planned more than a few hours or days in advance. Although she was enthusiastic about preparing this *Trilogy*, there were many demands on her time, and our schedules rarely coincided. For a woman in her eighties, she was remarkably vigorous, both physically and mentally, but her ability to reminisce, to recall fine details of the past, usually waned after thirty or forty minutes. She was still willing to talk, when time permitted, but after a half-hour or so her thoughts would drift into current happenings: visits to history meetings with Rupert N. Richardson; her latest community interests; her friends' fortunes or misfortunes, and so forth. Invariably, as she realized she had wandered from the subject, she would apologize—sometimes profusely. She was one of those rare persons who understand that even a historian's time can be limited and thrown into confusion by missed or delayed appointments.

Because of her sensitivity to my responsibilities on this project, I adjusted our meetings, and the working format for those meetings, in ways that would make them most productive for both of us. Thus we stuck to no rigid schedule. When she was in a mood to talk, we talked. When I was not available, she jotted down notes. When she was not available, I prepared question sheets for her to answer in writing. Sometimes she wrote on postal cards and on one occasion she wrote a nine-page letter. We conversed by telephone—at least once after midnight and once before breakfast. She wrote notes on the back pages of bridge scores, and frequently she wrote on paper napkins. She clipped newspaper articles and wrote comments on the margins. On one highly complimentary editorial in which Ed Wishcamper of the *Abilene Reporter-News* praised her generous philanthropies, she wrote: "This is *me* he's talking about!"—as if she could not quite believe she deserved such attention.

Mrs. Jones died before we could complete our project, and so it was left to me to decide how the material we had accumulated could best be shared with West Texans. I decided to allow Mrs. Jones to tell her own story insofar as is possible. Were she alive I can predict her reaction to my decision: first, she would be appalled; then there would be a few days of silent shock and bewilderment; later she would ask scores of questions; next, she would go to "Teacher" (Professor Rupert N. Richardson) who would reassure her; reluctantly she would give tentative approval; and finally she would be secretly pleased, although she would never show it. Her admiration for historians in general, and "Teacher" in particular, was genuine. This helped to write "our book" and to move her closer to that Ivory Tower of academia which her father and her mother's ancestors so admired.

Having made the decision to have her speak for herself, however, I was immediately confronted with a problem which at times seemed insurmountable: by holding to a chronological reproduction of our conversations, the resulting first draft of the manuscript lacked focus and direction. Statements appeared out of context and sometimes were incomprehensible. Many of her introductory statements had no historical value and would not hold the interest of the reader.

Reluctantly, I decided to develop an entirely new format: Without changing the meaning of a single word, and without rearranging the basic structure of a single sentence, I have reorganized and rewritten the entire manuscript. The responses are still those of Mrs. Jones—virtually *verbatim*. Their sequence has sometimes been changed and all discussions on a single topic have generally been grouped together. In some cases I have enlarged my original question so that the reader may more easily understand the context of Mrs. Jones's responses. Other minor changes have been made for smoother reading.

The reader should also be aware that many of our conversations occurred during the months just prior to the acceptance by the Texas A&M Press of my earlier manuscript on Judge Legett, Mrs. Jones's father, and continued for a year after its publication. I have included some of her comments during that period wherever I thought they helped the reader to better understand the varied interests of a remarkable woman.

CONVERSATIONS WITH RUTH LEGETT JONES
(Concerning her Grandmother Bryan)

Jones: Good morning.
Spence: Good morning.
Jones: I want you to be sure to appreciate my being here on time. I didn't read the *Wall Street Journal* or the *Dallas News*—not even Dear Abby—to make sure I wouldn't be late. I told the yard man as I was leaving I'd get here on time if it harelipped every cat in my alley.
Spence: What have you been doing lately?
Jones: Well, just this morning I had the nicest note from Miss Vaughn [director of the library at McMurry College] thanking me for the books I bought for McMurry, and she listed them every one. It was a warm, very appreciative letter.

I wrote and thanked her, like a good girl.

Maybe I hadn't told you that Teacher headed the committee that divided the money between the four Abilene libraries. They tried not to duplicate the books in the various libraries. Now isn't that nice?

Spence: Yes, indeed. Shall we talk about Granny Bryan?
Jones: Fire away.
Spence: Can you recall anything more [than I wrote in the biographical sketch] about Sophia's family, the Wyerses?
Jones: No, you have dug up more about them than I knew before. I only remember Granny Bryan and unfortunately I don't remember a whole lot about her.
Spence: Sophia was a middle-aged woman with grown children and a fairly settled life style in Falls County before the Bryans moved out to the frontier in 1885.
Jones: Yes.
Spence: Do you recall hearing any difficulty she encountered in adjusting to her new home and environment?
Jones: She liked it. Because she made herself like it. There wasn't anywhere else to go. There wasn't anything else to do. Everybody was in the same shape, or worse. If they wanted to prosper they went west. Granny, in her no nonsense way, had what is called "guts." When she had to, apparently she could do anything.

For example, she had quite a reputation for cutting her own cattle into, or out of, a herd. Somehow I never heard any of the family say that they thought that was extraordinary. And I'm sure it wasn't. She was not the kind to talk about it. We'd hear it more or less later; maybe around a camp fire when the whole family was out on one of the ranches.

One night I remember Granny laughing and saying that Colonel [Ruth Jones's grandfather, Colonel Washington Carroll Bryan] always knew he couldn't leave her because he knew she could rope her own horse, saddle it, and go into town looking for him. She would, too, if she had to. I don't believe Granny Bryan was afraid of anything, man or beast.

I can never remember Granny being affectionate, compassionate, forgiving, or patient. If you got yourself into a scrape, you got yourself out. Or else!
Spence: How would you describe Sophia's physical characteristics?
Jones: She was about average height. I guess about five feet,

four or five inches. Hair was very dark brown, but not quite black. She never had a gray hair to the day she died. Very straight hair. She had blue eyes. I don't remember the color of her eyes, but Mother once mentioned that all three of us [Sophia, Lora, Ruth] had blue eyes.

I can't remember anything else about the way she looked. What I remember most about Granny Bryan's appearance was great bundles of petticoats. Granny was always well-dressed, but I remember as a child thinking that all of her dresses looked alike . . . [after a brief hesitation] I shouldn't tell this. Edith and Judy [Jones's daughters] will kill me. But it's true! This story I heard many times about Granny, but I'll bet it happened to all the old ladies in their long skirts out in the country. On long drives there often came times when nature had to be answered. Now isn't that an unnecessary statement? Anyway, Granny had the most lady-like method of handling this. She would get out of the wagon, pretend to engage herself in raptures of a beautiful sunset, or a beautiful view, and stand very still for a few moments. Then, very slowly and sedately, she would move ahead and walk back to the wagon. *But,* there was always this slight, wet puddle where she had stood. Well, after all, a gal born to handle anything does the best she can. Right?

Go ahead and tell it if you want to, but I feel so gauche when I tell something like this. It sounds so un-Eastern Shore, doesn't it?

Spence: Would you like to make a bet that Eastern Shore ladies also receive calls from Mother Nature?

Describe for me Sophia's house in Abilene.

Jones: Two-story red brick, with a bright red roof, on South First. I remember the water from Catclaw Creek—which is usually bone-dry—being so high one time Judge [Jones's father] had to carry us across the street one at a time on horseback.

Spence: Were there any trees in the yard?

Jones: Now isn't that just like a Virginian to ask that question? The usual kind of West Texas trees. Nothing unusual or exciting about them.

Spence: No flowers?

Jones: Scrawny little things as I remember them.
Spence: Sophia Bryan, then, was not the kind of woman who liked to putter around in a flower garden?
Jones: Heavens no! I don't think she could have cared less. Maybe too many *important* things to worry about and to do.
Spence: So her yard wasn't exactly a botanical garden?
Jones: Oh, one year it was! Mother was so different, you see, and she could hardly stand it sometimes when Granny Bryan didn't have a thing in her yard. So, one spring Mother hauls Julia [Jones's sister] and me over there—Kade [Jones's brother] probably escaped as usual—and we worked like slaves. Flower beds everywhere, with azaleas, crepe myrtle, salt cedar, tamarisk, honeysuckle, bachelor's buttons, old maids, daisies, zinnias, roses, and chrysanthemums. In other words, just about everything that Mother could get her hands on.

I don't remember if she ever did it again. I know I didn't get caught again. When Mother had those bursts of energy I learned to find me a good hiding place.

Spence: What other recollections of the house do you have?
Jones: Well, as I said, it was two-story brick that looked like it started out with one idea in mind and then as it matured it changed its mind and direction several times. It wasn't very pretty, but it looked paid for. In those days that was the most important thing.

What I liked most about that house was: there were several culverts under which we children could hide our heavy coats on the way to school, and then get them on our way home—with poor, stupid parents not knowing any better. But one day Mother Nature fooled us and down came the darndest rain you ever saw. You guessed it: one coat was washed at least to the Gulf of Mexico and the other two were ruined. You know, Judge and Mother never did see anything funny about that. We didn't either after we recovered from our rear-end lickings.

Those coats, Julia's and mine, were yellow color with some long, white goat hair on them. I'm sure they smelled like a goat, too.
Spence: Describe the inside of Sophia's house as you remember it.

Jones: One of the things I remember most vividly was the upstairs bathroom. In fact, I can't recall there being any other bathroom in that whole house.

The tub was tin and boarded up on one side, with beaded ceiling boards, tub high. There was a window right over the middle of the tub that looked out over an unceiled attic, dark as old Billy. It was the eeriest, scariest, cobwebbiest looking place I ever saw, with dark shadows vaguely moving with any slight breeze. Lumpy-looking things that I am convinced to this day would move.

One time Granny had a sweet, very poor, country girl working for her and she would often give us our baths. She would get up to this horrible place before we got into the tub and hide. When we got undressed and into the tub, the girl made weird sounds, and moved and rattled something that sounded like an old chain—just like in the moving pictures. I am sure we broke a track record as three scared, cold, naked kids ran downstairs where the family was. We burst into the parlor where Granny and Colonel were entertaining somebody and yelled "Granny! Save us!" Granny and Colonel just laughed and laughed.

Incidentally, I can't ever remember being anything but cold in that tub.

Spence: Was water pumped up into the tub, or carried up by pail?

Jones: Carried up at first, as I remember, but then, wonder of wonders—when I was a child—it was pumped up to a tank in the attic and carried in from there. Cold! Cold!

Spence: How many bedrooms do you remember in Sophia's house?

Jones: I don't remember all the rooms, but four, maybe.

Spence: Did the house have both a living room and a parlor?

Jones: Both. But we weren't allowed very often in the parlor. I do remember the plush look of the upholstery in there, though.

Spence: Was there a dining room, or did everyone eat in the kitchen?

Jones: Granny had a funny-like looking, dreary dining room.

Everyone ate mostly in the kitchen. The dining room was mostly used as a passage from the kitchen.

Spence: It looks like our time is up today. I assume you will behave yourself until our next conversation.

Jones: Don't assume too much. I thought historians didn't do that sort of thing. Oh, no.

I wish we had more time but I promised to go out this morning with Teacher and the Wagstaffs [Robert and Texas] and a fine young man named Duane Hale to look at an old Spanish smelter. Mr. Hale has taken his master's at Abilene Christian University under Dr. Ralph Smith; his thesis is on these Spanish smelters.

Sounds fun, doesn't it, but don't tell me to behave. Don't you want me to have any fun, ever? I never saw anybody having fun behaving, but I'll look again . . . Oh, that reminds me of something:

Did I ever tell you the story about Teacher and me going down to San Antonio to some history meeting—maybe the Texas Philosophical—and Teacher goes up to the desk at the hotel and says in his big booming voice that we have reservations. The bright-looking young man behind the desk says, "One room?" Teacher says, loud enough to be heard across the lobby: "No. Two rooms. Two rooms. But make them as close together as possible." Oh, my. As innocent as a babe in the woods.

* * *

Spence: Good morning. Are you ready to confess all your past sins again today?

Jones: You really are a mess. If anybody had told me I would talk this much to anybody about anything I would have thought they were crazy. Now, where did we leave off?

Spence: We talked mostly about Sophia's house on South First Street. But tell me what Ruth Jones has been doing since our last meeting.

Jones: Well, my study group is enrolled again for the new

semester. McMurry College inherited us this year. Ruth Gay, Beth Duff, Mrs. Justin—and Ruth Williamson might join us—are all in Dr. Ungvary's course on African Studies. Or some such title. I'll be doing well this time if I can learn how to pronounce his name and get the title of the course right. I know it will be rough for all of us. It will be our first exposure to Hungarian Bulla-woola.

I felt so sorry for one young man sitting in class with a patch on the seat of his pants. But Beth said they buy them from the store that way!

Did I ever tell you that Katharyn Duff calls our study group "the floating crap game?"

And I wanted to tell you this. I think you'll appreciate it as I did: A Mr. Barnes, who is an associate pastor at St. Paul Methodist Church, and, I think he said, director of the youth program, came to call on us at the office the other day. He is the one who wrote us those nice letters about your first book [*Colonel Morgan Jones: Grand Old Man of Texas Railroading*], and he asked to see the Colonel's little trunk that you mentioned in the book. Well we opened it up for him while he was here, and there were the Old Mahn's [Colonel Morgan Jones's] soiled, discolored, and stiff collars just as he left them when he died in 1926. Mr. Barnes was so genuinely interested that I broke down and gave him one of the collars that had a MJ laundry mark on it, size 17½. Had I presented him with a marvelous gift, Mr. Barnes couldn't have appreciated it any more. Said he was going to use it as a book mark in your book about the Old Mahn.

Spence: I suppose you and I would appreciate that story more than anyone else.

Jones: I reckon . . . and I almost forgot something else: A Mr. Carpenter from Texas Tech called just this morning and asked to come by the office. He wanted to microfilm the Morgan Jones papers. I told him I would see you today and if there was no reason that you wanted to keep them here any longer, that Texas Tech could have the originals. They will make film copies for our files here.

Spence: I have copies myself, so I would have no further need of the originals.

Jones: Well, I'll just kiss the Morgan Jones papers good-bye. Mel [Melvin Holt, office manager] can send them on their way. I am sure Mr. Carpenter will take care of them.
Spence: Any university should be glad to have them.
Jones: You know, I've just decided to offer the Old Mahn's trunk to Grant Jones's boy [State Senator Grant Jones is her nephew] who is the only named Morgan Jones relative I know of.

Oh—I'm never going to give you time to talk about Granny—I must tell you one more thing: I heard a story on the Old Mahn the other day from one of the Pechaceks of Lion Hardware. They all used to know the Old Mahn very well. Gilbert Pechacek, I believe, used to eat breakfast with him quite often. He said he would never forget some of the things the Old Mahn said to him during those breakfasts, but one piece of advice in particular, he claimed, had saved him lots of money. Lion Hardware was just opening at the time and the Old Mahn felt the need to caution Gilbert about creditors—or rather, extending credit. He said, when a man came in asking for credit, Johnnie must check three things: One, if he had mud on his shoes; two, if he had paint on his pants; three, if he had a Bible under his arm. If he found *any* of those three things, *refuse* to extend him credit. Wise! Wise! Wise!

Now, what was it we were saying about Granny Bryan?
Spence: We've talked about her house and her yard, so now tell me what you remember about the ranches and ranch houses Colonel Bryan and Sophia owned.
Jones: I remember going to the ranch house near Hamlin a few times. One time we were almost there—an all day drive of about sixty miles—and Granny, who was driving the buggy, stopped the horses. Sudden like. I remember to this day: she silently pointed to a snake with her buggy whip and, without saying a word, got out of the buggy, grabbed the snake before it could coil, and popped his head with one quick snap of her arm and wrist. Later, the cowboys at the ranch told me Granny could do that most any time. Do you suppose she would break the snake's neck? Does a snake have a neck? Anyway, that snake

didn't feel so hot after that. Granny hung it on the barbed-wire fence, a common practice in those days.

Spence: Let's take Sophia in the house now. I mention in the biographical sketch that she didn't like to cook. But do you remember if she was a good cook when she finally got in the kitchen? Did she make cookies for you, Kade, and Julia, for example?

Jones: I don't recall seeing Granny Bryan in *any* kitchen *anywhere.* She and Colonel always had some terribly fat or terribly skinny girl in the kitchen who was practically a slave—as customs go now. But Grandmother Legett [her paternal grandmother] always had beautiful brown sugar biscuits. Get the picture?

Spence: Yes. Well, so much for Sophia's cooking. Do you have an impression, or specific recollection, that Colonel Bryan ever consulted her on business matters?

Jones: I know he did. I remember one time in particular when it impressed me tremendously as a youngster. It was during a drought and Colonel had to give away about fifteen hundred—I could be way off on the number—cattle. It was one of the dry, dry years. He gave five hundred to Judge, five hundred to Uncle Sam. Colonel and Granny worried and worried and talked and talked about it. They looked quite old and worn—to me—after the cattle were distributed. You see, they were upset because the cattle were suffering so, without enough water or grass. And, besides, they didn't want to give up so much of their herd.

Spence: Can you think of any other evidence that suggests that Sophia was interested in family business matters?

Jones: Well, she always wore the money belt and kept the family's cash. There were no banks and Colonel knew he would be robbed if *he* carried it, so Granny was elected. I saw that belt many-a-time; it was leather brown, muchly used-looking, with slots for different sizes of gold pieces.

Spence: Did she wear the money belt all day?

Jones: It was kept at home, but when Granny left the house she wore it. Her saddle was a side-saddle, naturally, with a railing around the side and back, and her rifle was strapped just below it by her right arm. She would say she hadn't had to use it very often because all the Indians and desperados knew she could shoot straight. Wish I knew where that rifle is. Couldn't it tell some tall tales?

Spence: Do you know whether Sophia Bryan ever actually used her gun?

Jones: Why, honey, I know she did. This story is one of the oldies. It has been told so many times it has to be true: Granny and her three little children—this was in Falls County, of course—were at the T-Diamond ranch and two outlaws came riding up about dark: thieves, cattle rustlers, or just plain ordinary outlaws. They asked for something to eat. Granny refused at first, but finally let them persuade her. She let them in, fed them, and then they demanded her money. She made out like she was terrified, but went to get the sugar for the coffee. She kept the sugar in the wardrobe under lock and key. But so was her gun in the wardrobe.

Then, all of a sudden, she came out of the wardrobe with both barrels a-blazing—so to speak—and said, "If you don't get out of here *now* and *fast* I'll put a hole in you so big a dog can crawl through!" Needless to say, they *did*. This saying has stood us in good stead all through the years.

Spence: But in that case Sophia used her gun without shooting it. You have said she was a "straight-shooter"; can you think of an actual case when she proved it?

Jones: Oh, yes; a scary one, too. I grew up being scared to death of mad dogs. This story didn't help any. Granny always said it was the dumbest thing she ever did. This was in Falls County, too, I guess, because her children were still small. Colonel had gone off on a cattle-buying trip. Granny was ill with an enormously swollen foot, barely able to hobble around the house, when their dog suddenly went into convulsions, frothing at the mouth, running wildly under the house. Granny could see the dog, but from inside she couldn't get a straight shot, so she hobbles out of the house, carrying the rifle. She finally gets a bead on the dog. She was lying down flat on the ground to get a

clean shot. While she was trying to get herself propped up, it suddenly occurred to her that if the dog had come out and made a run at her she wouldn't have time to shoot.
Spence: But she did shoot in time.
Jones: [Nodding affirmatively] Dead dog. End of story.
Spence: You mentioned, a few minutes ago, Sophia's sidesaddle. Did she always ride sidesaddle?
Jones: Except when nobody was looking.
Spence: Did she expect all women in her family to do likewise?
Jones: Absolutely. Even when Julia and I were young'uns we rode sidesaddle just like Granny. She would have been a disgrace to Colonel if she had ridden stride *in public*. Julia and I just barely did make the breakthrough about the time we were grown, and even then Kade and Judge felt disgraced. Kade even threatened to leave home he was so humiliated. Of course Julia was Miss Milktoast and left me to fight them alone. Mother found a dressmaker who knew how to make the divided skirts yards and yards wide. And I mean yards and yards!
Spence: You seem to remember Sophia as a typical pioneer woman, and yet it isn't likely that the typical pioneer mother would allow her eighteen-year-old daughter to go halfway across the country to a Virginia college. Isn't it possible that Sophia was less provincial—or perhaps less awed—by distant places than the typical pioneer woman?
Jones: I don't think that Granny was awed by anything much; but maybe I wasn't old enough to recognize a good awe when I saw one. I think Congressman Roger Q. Mills was living in Virginia, and a great friend of Colonel's and Granny's. Granny thought Mills could save any situation concerning her daughter [Lora] that had to be saved. I do know that Mother went to his home when Wesleyan Female Institute was temporarily closed or quarantined because of diptheria or scarlet fever.
Spence: So, you are sticking to your statement that Sophia was a fairly typical woman on the frontier?
Jones: Unflappable, maybe? That's what I think I mean.
Spence: Why didn't your Aunt Julia [Sophia's older daughter] go to college?

Jones: She fell in love *early* with Uncle Sam. Now *there* was a character of all characters. The most colorful person in the family, I guess. Either cussing or laughing all the time. He said once if ladies' skirts were as short in his day as they were later, son-of-a-gun, they'd have to shoot him. He said he once caught a glimpse of Aunt Julie's ankle—that's before they were married—and he couldn't sleep for a week. Born without a dime, and had no education, but loved by all the family. Always claimed to be kin to General [Nathaniel] Greene of New England history.

Spence: I want to hear more about him, when we talk about Lora's generation.

Jones: I don't think I could dare repeat it even if I did think of something else he said.

Spence: Back to Sophia: Did she ever read to you when you were a child, or show any interest in reading to herself?

Jones: I never saw or heard Granny Bryan read to any of her grandkids. Never saw her read a book.

Spence: Do you suppose you've just forgot?

Jones: No, I just doubt that she could read that well, or had the time or interest for it.

Spence: Since you were the youngest of Lora's children, did you feel that you might have been Sophia's favorite grandchild?

Jones: Heavens, no! Julia and Kade were her favorites.

Spence: You seem so sure.

Jones: You'd better put a pinch of salt on what I say about this part of Granny.

Julia was pretty, cute, cuddly, and sweeter than I was. Kade was the only grandson at that time. I didn't blame Granny, and didn't much care; as long as I had my horse Nell I didn't need anybody or anything else. Granny just didn't have time for me or vice versa. But when Granny wanted something, I was the first one she called. Mother understood this, I think, and tried to make up for Granny. Sounds like I didn't like Granny, but I did. She just wasn't a very mushy or affectionate person. Life for her was pretty matter-of-fact and realistic.

Spence: Your own keen sense of humor is one of your outstanding personality traits, and yet it seems that Sophia had no sense of humor at all.

Jones: Not much, as I recall. Maybe I don't remember. I *do* remember that Colonel had a sense of humor. His frequent expression was "Dod dimmit." That was the strongest language, or the nearest to cussing, he ever got. I never heard any man in my family use cuss words: Judge, Colonel, and Old Mahn, Uncle John . . . oh, oh, now that I think more about it, maybe I had better exclude Uncle Sam. He wouldn't fit on *anybody's* no-cussing list. But Uncle Sam, like all the rest, seemed to have a strong sense of honor around women. All of them had a strong sense of humor, too; more ribald than clever, as I remember. But Uncle Sam . . . oh, my.

Spence: Back to Sophia. Now this might be difficult, but try to respond to it anyway: What sweeping generalizations could you make about Sophia Wyers Bryan, either from your own recollections or from impressions you have picked up from older members of the family?

Jones: Now what kind of question is that?

Spence: Do you wish I would stop being so nosey?

Jones: Yes! But let's see . . .

Spence: Try just once to put Sophia Wyers Bryan in a nutshell.

Jones: I guess I just don't feel qualified to voice an opinion. Maybe the thread that runs all through Granny's generation to mine is: expecting and wanting to be somebody. Second-class anything didn't fit into her scheme of things. Everybody better measure up, or else!

Spence: This might be another difficult one: What would you say is the most obvious difference between Sophia Bryan and her granddaughter Ruth Jones?

Jones: [After several moments of studied thought] I guess it would be this: When a mad dog ran through Granny's yard, she got out her gun and shot it. If I saw a mad dog running through my yard, I would get out a gun and shoot myself.

Spence: Not bad. One more question of this "nosey" type. I want to go back to something you said a few minutes ago: You don't look upon yourself as Sophia's favorite grandchild. Now that you are an adult, can you explain it to your own satisfaction?

Jones: I just didn't rate too well with Granny, but I do understand and thought I had explained it: Kade was the oldest grandson. Julia was a cuddly, not very strong little girl. On the other hand, I was not the sweet, lap-sitting kind. My legs and arms were too long from the day I was born.

Spence: So it would seem that you look upon Sophia Wyers Bryan as somewhat typical of the frontierswoman—unflappable, you said—but you don't think that she would fit any of the stereotypes. She was not a Calamity Jane . . .

Jones: No.

Spence: . . . she was not a saloon girl with a heart of gold . . .

Jones: No, but wouldn't we have fun talking about her if she had been.

Spence: She was not a frontier suffragist . . .

Jones: Never.

Spence: . . . and she was not a silent saint in a sunbonnet?

Jones: That least of all.

Spence: Then what was she?

Jones: I thought you said no more questions like that. [After a few moments of deep thought]: Independent, but not in the liberationist style. Self-sufficient, although I doubt she ever thought about self-sufficiency one way or the other. I guess she was just a rancher's wife with ambition for herself and more ambition for her children. Wealthier, I guess, in land and cattle.

Spence: She suffered no great physical hardship or privation on the frontier?

Jones: Maybe as a child in east Texas, yes, I suppose she did. But when she moved out here, I never heard of any hardship.

Spence: Would you guess she was a typical rancher's wife?

Jones: Beats me. It looks like I've run out of soap.

Spence: Do you remember when Sophia died?

Jones: Oh, yes. It doesn't seem like she was sick very long, but she must have been.

Spence: Do you remember the ailment that killed her?

Jones: I think she died of kidney trouble. Bright's disease.

Spence: One more question: Can you recall any activity in which Sophia was engaged that was entirely separate from her family or home?

Jones: Remember, in her day there were hardly any women who did anything unrelated to family or home. No, I don't imagine Granny ever established her own image or even thought that she should have her own image.

Spence: O.K. Fine. I think we've done a good day's work.

Jones: I feel like I've died on the vine, but I want to tell you about another project of mine. Do you have time?

Spence: Forever.

Jones: I have been doing some excavation on an accumulation of over fifty years of housekeeping, and now, as a result, I have given away sixty years' of *National Geographics* to Abilene Christian University—from 1912 on to last month's.

I've given to Abilene Community Theatre dozens of boxes of lovely old evening dresses—costumes of all kinds for plays. I am now in the process of going through three floors of my library. The whole house is covered with small piles and big piles of books, either going up to the second or third-floor bookcases, or coming down. You see, part of them I had decided to give to the University Women's book auction, but every day I go back and take some and put them back in my shelves. I really can't bear to part with any of them. I'll never get through.

I found one book from England with the date 1728. I found another book which had written on the fly leaf: "To my good friend Gen. Sam Houston, from blank, blank"—haven't figured out the name yet. Looks like Sassoon, 1850. I found another *Tatler* sheet dated 1697; several more books printed in the 1700s; a set of *History of Our Country,* number 301 of a collection of only five hundred printed. Gorgeous colored plates in them by a man named Eillis. Any one of the plates would make an excellent framing. A set of Luther Burbank books—he died the same day the Old Mahn did—with more beautiful colored plates. Twelve volumes, I believe. My literary cup runneth over.

Spence: How did you happen to own one of Sam Houston's books?

Jones: You would never guess in a million years. I was in Fence Houses, in England, many years ago, visiting Mrs. T.C. Jones, and I saw a shelf of books behind the kitchen stove in Percy's [Ruth Jones's husband] mother's house. Of course we'll never know for sure how it came to be there, but don't you imagine that the Old Mahn took it to England with him on one of his trips and gave it to one of the family?

Spence: It sounds like a good possibility.

Jones: I took the book with me last week-end to Houston because Llerene Friend, of Austin, who wrote that marvelous book on Sam Houston, was to be there at the Institute of Letters meeting. She had a small tizzy over it.

Oh, I just remembered another of Uncle Sam's favorite sayings; one that I can quote in fairly polite company: One time he drove a herd of cattle from here to Abilene, Kansas,—before there was an Abilene, Texas—and apparently it snowed all the way. As he told us the story many years later he said that he "slept in the damn-golly snow" every night on the drive. I said, "Uncle Sam, where did you pick up that saying?" Well, he says, Aunt Julie was always reprimanding him for saying damn when there was company in the house, and she says if he must swear he ought to say "golly." Well, he could never remember to say golly until he had already said damn, so he just decided to do the best he could with damn-golly.

I'm limp from talking so much, and its your fault.

PART TWO

"Mrs. Legett, I think I see your children in the tree."

LORA BRYAN LEGETT (1867-1923)

LORA BRYAN LEGETT
(1867-1923)

Lora Bryan Legett was born in Falls County, Texas, November 6, 1867, to Sophia Wyers Bryan and Washington Carroll Bryan. She had an older brother, John, and an older sister, Julia. Lora's ancestors on both sides of her family were tillers of the soil. They migrated west during the early national period in American history: the Wyerses from Pensylvania and the Bryans from North Carolina. Lora's maternal ancestors showed an uncommon interest in education for women and were among the founders of Wesleyan Female Institute in Staunton, Virginia, and Waco Female College in Waco, Texas. Lora's father—who farmed in Tennessee and worked as a blacksmith in Mississippi as a young man—established a cattle and cutting-horse ranch in Falls County, Texas, following military service as a Texas Ranger and as a Confederate Army colonel during the Civil War.

After a year of study at each of the two colleges founded by her maternal ancestors, Lora Bryan moved with her family in 1885 to Abilene, in central West Texas. Abilene was the nearest town on the Texas and Pacific rails to her father's ranch lands in Jones, Fisher, Stonewall, and Taylor counties. The poised and pretty eighteen-year-old, who had a natural talent in art, and who had been trained at the two colleges to appreciate music, poetry, literature, and drama, immediately attracted the attention of Abilene's Beau Brummels. Lora's attention, in turn, eventually centered upon twenty-eight-year-old K.K. Legett, a self-educated, but highly competent lawyer. Legett, who had moved to Buffalo Gap, Texas, only four years earlier, was one of Abilene's founders. Only one year before Lora's arrival in Abilene, young Legett had served as a presidential elector from Texas in the election of Grover Cleveland.

Lora Bryan married K.K. Legett June 10, 1886, and in time they were the parents of one son, Kade, and two daughters, Julia and Ruth.

As wife and mother, Lora was not a typical frontierswoman. To a far greater degree than the average woman on the American frontier, Lora was, like her mother before her, an equal partner in family business matters. Family records strongly suggest that she served as her husband's consultant and confidante as they rapidly accumulated thousands of acres of West Texas land. Whenever a decision had to be made between a purchase of more land or an investment in more and better creature-comforts, Lora almost always encouraged her husband to increase their farm and ranch land holdings.

Lora Legett's attention did not center exclusively, however, upon her husband's rapidly expanding business enterprises. Her day-to-day routine on the edge of the Texas frontier also included her children's training in education, music, and home responsibilities. In addition, she practiced at all times the polished good manners and hospitality of a Southern lady. She expected nothing less from her two daughters.

At home Lora held firmly to the conviction that cleanliness is next to godliness. With some assistance from her children, and sporadic help from various housekeepers and yardmen (almost all of whom could never match her energy and drive), she cleaned the henhouse, dipped the chickens (in a carbolic acid solution to kill bluebugs), swept the sidewalks, dusted the furniture (every piece curled and carved in the best dust-catching, Victorian style), washed dishes, spaded the garden, picked and strung beans, shelled peas, shucked corn, dug potatoes, picked berries, and made lye soap. Churning was the worst job of all and, therefore, according to the young frontier mother, "the best character-builder" ever devised for growing children.

In the community, Lora Legett accepted her share of duties for the Ladies Aid Society at the First Baptist Church and for various other social organizations, such as the Abilene Shakespearean Club.

When she had a few spare minutes alone, Lora would enter her private world of art, music, and literature. Her paintings were sometimes good enough to win blue ribbons at the county fair; her familiarity with Honore de Balzac, Sir Walter Scott, and William Cullen Bryant enabled her to quote with confidence long passages to her children at appropriate intervals throughout the day; and her love of music was so strong that she once had three grand pianos in her parlor, unable to choose between them.

As her children approached their early 'teen years, Lora Legett and her husband planned, designed, and built—with the assistance of a Dallas builder—a palatial home in the 600 block of Meander Street in south Abilene. Newsmen thereafter referred to it as the "Legett mansion." Mrs. Legett devoted the remainder of her life to her role as a competent and vivacious matriarch of the Legett home. The mansion became a beehive of social, educational, and religious activity. It was the gathering place for business and political leaders from around the state, and the axis around which her children's social life revolved. During their high school years the mansion was the focal point for parties and lawn picnics; later, when the children returned for holidays from colleges in Indiana, Tennessee, and Virginia, the home filled with school friends from all sections of the nation.

Lora Legett hosted numerous social affairs during the course of a year: an annual Christmas reception for which the entire first floor was decorated with cranberries and candles and a stringed orchestra stationed on the stairway landing; an annual New Year's open house (for which the orchestra returned); an annual Thanksgiving Day dinner for close relatives; annual luncheons for the XYZ Club and the Abilene Shakespearean Club; and more numerous luncheons and business meetings for the Ladies Aid Society.

Thus Lora Bryan Legett adapted as easily as her mother to the West Texas frontier and worked even more diligently to smooth its rough edges. By drawing upon her education and training in east Texas and Virginia schools, and upon other varied interests and experiences made possible by enlightened, affluent, and relatively indulgent parents, Lora contributed significantly to the lives of those around her. As mother, church worker, and social leader, she was a vital part of the process of changing a wild-and-woolly West Texas frontier saloon town into a vigorous and progressive little city. Even before the turn of the century, Abilene, Texas—less than two decades old—was noted in the Southwest for its uncommon educational, religious, and social achievements. Lora Bryan Legett's presence there accounted for a considerable portion of that success.

CONVERSATIONS WITH RUTH LEGETT JONES
(Concerning her mother, Lora Legett)

Spence: Good morning.
Jones: Good morning to you. I *knew* leading a pure, clean life wouldn't pay, and sure enough it hasn't. I've been in and out of the hospital for about two weeks—an infection of "unknown origin." Isn't that ridiculous? It started with an infected nail in a manicure, turned into a run-around and then did various other funny things. Now I'm wobbly and cross as a bear. They gave me tons of antibiotics. Had to miss my new history class out at Simmons, and when I go back I won't have the least idea what they are talking about.
Spence: So the "floating crap game" moved to Hardin-Simmons this semester.
Jones: Didn't I tell you? Mickey Haynie and I are the only members this time; the others chickened out. We are auditing a course from Dr. Aston called "Briton Yesterday and Today." It is very interesting, but at eight o'clock in the *morning!* Oh, my. I guess Mickey and I are the chickens since we are the only ones who are foolish enought to get up that early.
Spence: Did you and Dr. Richardson attend the Western Historical Association meeting this year?
Jones: Of course. Dr. and Mrs. Astin and the Lewises went with us. We left Tuesday afternoon and came back on Sunday afternoon. I am full of old facts, new facts, and things in general. Had a grand time.

Spence: Did you behave?
Jones: Well, I'm not sure. I don't think Teacher thought so. You see, I ran Mr. Wardlaw [Frank Wardlaw, former director of the Texas A&M Press] to earth. This was after you revised your *Judge Legett* manuscript for him, remember. So, I nonchalantly sauntered by the A&M Press book exhibit and—behold!—there *he* was, bigger than life. Wonder why Teacher won't believe me when I tell him it was a coincidence?

Anyway, Mr. Wardlaw called me by name and said how glad he was to see me, asked about you, and so forth. I answered his questions fairly clearly, I hope, and stumbled on.

When I recovered a little—maybe ten minutes—I made a mighty resolve. I turned around, went back and asked him to come buy me a drink, or I'd buy him one. Teacher was nowhere around, understand. He [Wardlaw] told his assistant that he had known me for twenty or thirty years. Imagine that. I told him that that was long enough acquaintance for us to have our first drink together. So here we went—two Bloody Marys apiece before noon. I told him how often I had heard of him and gushed about his publications. Otherwise we talked about the weather and the excellence of the Bloody Marys. Just between us, they were terrible.

I confessed a little bit of this to Teacher—but like it was an accidental meeting—and he said he thinks I should stay out of the picture on account of your manuscript will stand on its own. He says after reading your revision there isn't a chance that Wardlaw won't be interested in publishing it.

Teacher was intimating rather bluntly, you see, that I was cluttering the "book-scape." So, I guess I didn't behave. I hope I haven't messed things up for you. Oh, dear.
Spence: Of course you didn't. He will not publish it if it doesn't measure up. Who else did you see at the meeting?
Jones: We saw Dr. Athearn [Robert G. Athearn, Professor of History at the University of Colorado] but never close enough to speak to.

I almost forgot to tell you the highlight! Teacher got an award of merit that pleased him immensely. Entirely unex-

pected. A complete surprise to both of us. They awarded it at the Friday night dinner where the governor of Colorado spoke.
Spence: Are you ready to talk about your mother for awhile?
Jones: Any time, I'm ready to talk about Mother.
Spence: I brought with me this copy of the original newspaper [*Abilene Reporter*] account of Lora Bryan's marriage to K.K. Legett. Would you read it, so we could then talk about it?
Jones: Oh, goody! It's so long, and all on the front page!
[NOTE: The major portion of the article datelined June 11, 1886, follows, so that the reader can share this excellent example of pioneer efforts to bring social refinement to the raw frontier. Abilene, Texas, was just five years and three months old at that time. The wedding was more than a social affair; it provided "respectable" entertainment for the entire town.]

GOLDEN BELLS
MISS LORA BRYAN AND MR. K.K. LEGETT
Ceremonies at the Church—Costumes Elegant
Good Wishes and Good Cheer

At an early hour last evening every seat in the spacious Presbyterian church was filled in anticipation of one of the happiest events in this city—the marriage of Miss Lora Bryan and Mr. K.K. Legett. By 8 o'clock p.m. the edifice was filled to its utmost capacity by lady and gentleman friends of the contracting parties, and those who had delayed their arrival drew their carriages up to the windows and gazed through the casement upon the animating scene within.

The altar at the southern end of the auditorium was gracefully festooned with immortels and supported two handsome vases filled with choice exotics. In front of and flanking the altar were three exquisitely carved, marble-topped tables, the central one of which supported an antique urn that blushed with a profusion of rare flowers and from which fell waving lines of green. The tables to the right and left were also tastefully decorated with flowers. Immediately in front of these, in the space between the tables and first line of seats, was erected a large evergreen arch with one base toward the pulpit and the other resting at the foot of the first line of the auditorium. From the center of this arch depended a large horseshoe ingeniously fashioned out of flowers and arbor-vitae.

Over the points where the two aisles lead stood two massive evergreen arches, from the southern one of which was suspended the floral letter "B" signifying that the bride would pass under it as Miss Bryan, and from the northern arch depended the letter "L," through which, after the ceremony, she would pass as Mrs. Legett.

At 9:15 o'clock the carriages of the bridal party drew up at the western door of the church and formed into line. Miss May De Allison, of Longview, and Mr. E.G. Senter, of Fort Worth, headed the line; next came Miss Anna Bass and Hon. G.A. Kirkland, both of Abilene; third, Miss Eugenie McDonald, of Marlin and Mr. John Bryan, of Abilene, and these were followed by the bride and groom elect.

The bride wore an elegant dress of surrah silk and brocaded satin, entraine; low corsage and elbow sleeves, embroidered in seed pearl, flounced down the front with point lace. Ornaments, natural flowers and diamonds.

Miss May De Allison was attired in a dress of white lace and mull; blue sash and ribbons, diamond ornaments.

Miss Anna Bass wore white oriental lace and mull; pink sash and ribbons, diamond ornaments.

Miss Eugenie McDonald, cream satin and oriental lace, diamond ornaments.

At 9:20 Mrs. Cora Young touched the organ

with skillful fingers and to the rich melody of Mendelsohn's wedding march the bridal party swept down the western aisle and thence along the southern aisle, through the arch from which depended the letter "B." The bridesmaids took positions in front of the altar, while the groomsmen stood opposite. The fair bride and happy bridegroom stood between, and under the horseshoe which hung suspended from the central arch. Rev. L.H. Cheney took position opposite the contracting parties and spoke the words that made Lora Bryan and K.K. Legett man and wife. Soft fell the light of chandeliers upon the two who were linking their destinies for the journey of life and for, perhaps, a happy eternity. Flowers breathed sweet incense and the hushed audience listened in breathless silence to the words of the minister, who asked the usual questions and then said in a clear and firm voice: "According to the laws of God and this commonwealth, I pronounce you man and wife." Rev. Mr. Chaney implored the divine blessing and once more the deep voice of the organ pealed joyously forth.

The bridal party fled from the church and repaired to the Bryan residence in the western portion of the city. No cards had been issued, but about one hundred of the immediate friends of the bride and groom assembled at the residence and wished them a long and happy journey over the sunlet sea of married life.

A magnificent supper was spread in the dining room and the happy twain were pledged in sparkling cups of generous wine. After the banquet, the guests repaired to the drawing rooms where music and pleasant conversation sped the hours on rosy wings . . .

Jones: Oh, my. Adjectives and adverbs were certainly popular in those days. But I like it, don't you?

Spence: Yes, indeed. Eastern folks would have been amazed to

know how quickly the pioneer women brought civilization to the frontier. Do you still have Lora's wedding gown?
Jones: Yes, I do.
Spence: Would you describe it?
Jones: Well, you have to remember that hers was one of the first weddings in Abilene. Probably the first formal church wedding, but of course I'm not sure of that. I believe somebody has told me that, though. Ruth [Bradfield] Gay used to make much over the fact that the dress was made in Kentucky and cost more than a hundred dollars.

The train was a white brocaded satin, as the paper said, but now it has turned a beautiful golden color. She wore the train from her waist. Very few women could have done that at her height. She wasn't as tall as I am, but carried herself beautifully. The train must have been ten or twelve feet long. I never thought to measure it. It seems to me like she'd have to have two or three pages or bridesmaids to help her carry it, but I never heard her say. Her cap was outlined in seed pearls, as the paper says, and so were her slippers. The dress itself was more or less the usual "that age" type of dress.
Spence: Is there anything else you want to say about the wedding?
Jones: Well, the dress really was ornamented with seed pearls and diamonds, but hadn't you better say brilliants or something? Diamonds sound like we might be over-doing it, don't you think?
Spence: No. Remember what Teacher says: stick with the truth. I can't remember seeing a picture of Lora prior to her marriage. Does one exist?
Jones: Not that I know of. Isn't that awful?
Spence: Yes, for both of us. Do you recall any descriptions of her by those who knew her as a 'teen-ager, or when she first came to Abilene in 1885?
Jones: I have often heard people who knew her when she was a young woman say that she was most attractive, quite stylish-looking and dressing, and *very* popular.
Spence: Do you recall any mention of her courtship days?

Jones: No . . . oh, yes I do, too, and I never go to Buffalo Gap that I don't take my hat off to the big old mountain off to the west [Callihan Divide] where she said Judge first told her he loved her. There is a lovely view of the mountain at sundown when Teacher and I go to Buffalo Gap for dinner. I think of Judge and Mother every time we pass it. But that's about all I remember. You pointed out in the Legett manuscript that they frequently went to the opera house.

Spence: Let's begin, then, with a quick character sketch of Lora Bryan Legett as you remember her from childhood. Begin anywhere.

Jones: Mother had a keen, bubbly sense of humor, gay, energetic to a fault, industrious, ambitious, eager for more culture in our town and in her own life.

Her favorite hobby was reading. Balzac. Thackeray to a lesser degree. Scott she loved. Dickens she tolerated. But William Cullen Bryant was her love in life and she was forever quoting the line about the "door that swings between forever and no more."

One of my most vivid memories of Mother was dipping the old hens when she cleaned the hen house—which she did far too often. We young'uns had to catch the hens for her, and she dipped them in carbolic solution that she had to be very careful about not getting in their eyes. I can hear her laugh now about the difference in the hens, who submitted docilely, and the old roosters who squawked to high heaven. Mother would say, "Isn't that just like men?" and would laugh and laugh.

She and dirt were natural enemies. She would sweep the long walks—and I do mean long—every day, and even clean up the spare bedrooms when they hadn't been used all week.

She was a good cook, but often she didn't help her best dishes by our having to "use up something" even if it didn't match the main dish at all. She could make the best caramel icing I have ever tasted to this day and I often got to lick the spoon! Her roast beef was especially good. We never had lamb in our house. She said she had it often enough at school in Virginia to last a lifetime.

Her favorite yardman was named Mr. Lamkin. He and she would go out to the garden, and while they worked they sang at the top of their voices which, I was always painfully sure, could be heard all over town. "Amazing Grace" was her favorite. "Just as I Am" was another favorite. Oh, yes, "In the Sweet Bye and Bye" they sang over and over and over again.

I should have mentioned—when she was sweeping those long walks she would sing and dance, keeping time with her broom strokes. Mother had a nice way of laughing at herself, and one of her favorite stories concerned swinging those brooms. One spring morning, as she swept, she began to hear her heart murmur and gurgle. It got to be right distressing. She felt all right, but she would go back to the house and lie down. Her heart would stop murmuring and gurgling at once, but as soon as she'd pick up that broom, there would go the murmur and gurgle again. It looked like she would have to stop sweeping, as much as she liked to clean. It was weeks, she said, before she discovered the problem. Her "heart trouble" was actually the water in the hollow broom handle, where rainwater had seeped into it and got trapped—gurgle, gurgle, gurgle.

I know more about this, but I'm afraid I've run out of time. Can we pick up here the next time?
Spence: Of course. We'll start with more about Lora's and Mr. Lamkin's yard work. I want to hear more about that.
Jones: I meant to tell you: Katharyn Duff has been in Buffalo Gap recently and she called the other day and asked me if I wanted to see Grandfather Legett's house. I told her I surely did. But she hemmed and hawed and said several times "Are you *sure*?" Well, it must be some kind of a hog pen neighborhood, but I am going to make her take me there just the same. And that reminds me:

You wrote in *Judge Legett* that the founders of Buffalo Gap [where Jones's Grandfather Legett lived for a few years] called the town "the uncrowned queen of the woolly West," and you even named the second chapter by that title. I don't think of Buffalo Gap as a "queen" or as "woolly," do you? I think of San Angelo, with its sheep and goats as woolly. Buffalo Gap seemed more hide and hair to me.

Spence: That's a good point. I'll look at that chapter title again before the book is published.

* * *

Jones: Good Morning. Sorry you haven't heard from the Texas A&M Press yet about *Judge Legett*. I believe publishers and doctors belong to the same system of mental torture—waiting to get them to pay attention to you—just to impress the poor suffering people.
Spence: You could be right.
Jones: If you haven't heard from Mr. Wardlaw by the time Teacher and I go to the TSHA [Texas State Historical Association] meeting later this month, maybe I'll pretend I'm sick and not go.
Spence: Why would you do that?
Jones: I'll be sure to get myself into trouble. I might let a hint slip out to Mr. Wardlaw. Or I might start nudging Teacher to say something. Now I didn't say that! Teacher would probably tell me, again, to mind my own business. He has a nice diplomatic way of putting me in my place, but he sees that I get the point. He's always right, of course.
Spence: Of course.
Jones: Before we start talking about Mother, I have a priceless story that I must share with you. As you know, Teacher and I eat at the Buffalo Gap Steak House almost every Saturday night. Most of the waitresses are older women—well, not half as old as we are, I guess—but older women who probably live out there at Buffalo Gap and, unfortunately, they still have to work to support themselves. Maybe they just don't want to sit home all the time and rock. I don't know.

Anyway, all of them are dear souls and I fall in love with every one of them. But this one in particular seemed to want to wait on us more than the usual. You see, they use paper napkins out at the steak house, but lately we've been given linen napkins. Neither of us noticed that the people at the other tables didn't have linen napkins. Finally, we did. As we were leaving I mentioned our linen napkins to the manager and his wife. It was last Saturday night. They explained quietly, so our waitress wouldn't hear and be embarrassed, that some time ago she asked if she could bring her own napkins from home for us to use. She explained that her children were all grown and gone and she rarely has company, and she just liked to see her beautiful napkins used; so every Saturday she brings them to work with her, puts them in a special drawer in the front office, and then gets them out when she sees us coming. Then, she takes them home, hand-launders them, and gets them ready for the next Saturday night.

Can you compete with that story? It is one of my choicest, and I'll love it always. I call it a precious bead on my rosary of memories. There will never be another bead on that rosary worth more than this one, even had it cost a million dollars.

Spence: That's a beautiful story. Do you mind if I include it in the *Trilogy?*

Jones: No, honey, go right ahead. Not even Teacher can object to that one.

Spence: At our last interview . . .

Jones: Conversation . . .

Spence: In out last conversation, we were talking about Lora and Mr. Lamkin.

Jones: He worked for Mother for years. In fact, he was the only one she could keep for any length of time. Mother never could keep much help, and for two reasons: One, there weren't that many household servants available; and two, Mother *could* and *did* work them down. She worked right along with them, though.

Spence: Let's switch to an entirely new subject: Did Lora like to dance?

Jones: She loved to dance; and I guess that is one of the surest tests of her great love for Judge, that she gave it up, at his insistence, when they got married. Before they were married Mother would sometimes go with one of the dancing instructors here to give exhibition dances. Could be that Judge was a little jealous.

Spence: Judge never danced, even as a bachelor?
Jones: You know, I never thought so, but he must have. Before they were married, I guess. Mother once told me about Judge getting so mad because she danced with Dr. Jim Alexander when Judge was listed next in her dance book. Mother said they had a real "set-to" later that night. It must have been while they were courting.
Spence: So Judge Legett didn't like Lora to dance. Did she dislike any of his pastimes?
Jones: Mother couldn't abide card games. Never played. Never tried to learn. But Judge enjoyed a pennyante poker game. He never did admit it though. Oh, no. I guess he didn't play very often. Didn't have time.
Spence: On another subject: The first home you remember as a child must have been the little one on Pine Street.
Jones: Yes. It was about four rooms, or so it seems. Abilene was still very young and very small, and Judge and Mother were saving every dime to buy more land. Land, land, and more land is what Mother thought about. The Pine Street house looked like a tenant farmer's and was not much better. A hydrant on the back porch was our water supply. No inside plumbing at all. We young'uns were bathed—"every Saturday night," I guess—in front of the old Majestic range, in a tin wash tub which had been filled with hot water from a tank in the back of the stove.

I hate to say this as a fact, but I think we were all bathed in the same water, then Mother would wash out our long underwear and our "Faye" stockings in that bath water.
Spence: Back up just a minute; what were "Faye" stockings?
Jones: Well, honey, they were the kind that buttoned onto our underwear; long, black cotton lisle, I think. *Ugly as sin!* Judge then emptied the tub of water on some plant of Mother's choosing. Mustn't waste any water. Oh, no.
Spence: What else can you recall about the Pine Street house?
Jones: There wasn't enough of it to remember much. It was not too far from the present campus of Simmons. I don't think there was another house between us and it. We had a couple of horses: Dundee and Kirk. Also a cow, some chickens, and a rab-

bit. The same rabbit whose funeral you have described in your Legett manuscript.

That house was way out of the city limits, and very primitive. I think we moved from that to one on South First Street—maybe eight rooms in that one—west of the old high school. Funny but I don't remember much about that house except it was near Colonel and Granny Bryan's. We must have moved from there to the big, new house on Meander. Yes, I think we did.

Spence: Your father was very typical of the pioneer settler in the West whose financial successes eventually enabled him to build a house that was symbolic of his economic and social position in the community. As I prepared his biography I was especially impressed by the enormous time he spent overseeing the construction on Meander Street. As I've said before, newsmen always called it "the Legett mansion." The construction seemed to be all-consuming for about a year of his life.

Jones: Well, now that you mention it, I think maybe Mother should have been a more prominent person in that chapter. But of course your purpose was to write about Judge.

Spence: Could you mention more of the specific things she did in getting the house built and furnished?

Jones: You see, that's the point I meant to make. She did none of the actual building, but all of the furnishing. I really don't recall the many details of her preparations for that house, but I think you made it clear, yourself, that she did the planning: located a house style she liked, changed the interior to suit her and Judge's needs, and so on. Then Judge did the ordering and supervising—or meddling. But the only records that exist have to do with Judge's part of the work: the letters, the blueprints, for example. But I have just vague recollections of the exhaustive work Mother did of furnishing every room of that big house.

I am almost certain they furnished the Meander Street house with totally new furniture—well, with some exceptions, of course. I marvel that Judge and Mother let loose of so much money in such a brief time, but they must have planned that house for years and years and waited to do it only when they could afford it. Can you imagine having to sit down and order—sight unseen in many cases—so much furniture? But I do remember one thing: they were awfully proud of it when it was finished. I suspect Judge was even prouder than Mother, but he'd never admit it out loud.

Spence: It is obvious that you have a high regard for Lora Legett's housekeeping abilities. She was also good at giving her three children specific and continuing responsibilities around the house. Now, what about Judge Legett? Have you meant to give him no credit for the overall smooth running of the household?

Jones: Heavens, no! I was thinking we had already covered his part in your manuscript about him.

Spence: We'll have to assume that there will be some readers of *Trilogy* who have not read *Judge Legett of Abilene*, so perhaps you should give Judge some credit here, too.

Jones: As busy as Judge was in his office, on the farms and ranches, at Simmons, at Texas A&M where he served as chairman of their Boards, and so forth, I sometimes marvel that he still was able to do so much at home, but he did. He milked the cows, he cleaned out the lots and barn, he fed the horses, he did almost all of the lawn mowing, he kept the acetylene tank working—I guess we ought to say he worked around the house instead of in it. Of course, he always had Mr. Lamkin or somebody to help out, but Judge was like Mother, he worked harder at the job than the person hired to do it. Then, as you show in *Judge Legett of Abilene,* building the big house on Meander almost "done him in."

Spence: O.K., we'll give some of the credit to Judge for Lora's orderly household.

Jones: Yes, indeed, and maybe even some of the credit that people often gave instead to Mother. You know, for example, how hot it can get in Abilene in the summer time. Well, people were always saying to Mother that her house was so cool—even on the hottest days. It was always said like they were giving her credit. It was Judge, though, who insisted to the contractor who was building the house that he raise the ceilings a foot higher than the plans called for. I remember Judge talking about that many a time. He loved it, incidentally, when someone called it a mansion. Never admitted it of course.

But Judge was long since dead when Joe Williamson—whose family later bought the house—discovered that Judge had put great gobs of cotton up in the attic to absorb the heat. That must have been long before anybody ever thought of insulation.

Spence: Our time is up again. Are you planning a big weekend?

Jones: Teacher, the Wagstaffs, and I are going to Fort Parker this Friday and then back by Glen Rose to see the dinosaur tracks. Something I've wanted to see forever. And by the way, did you know that Jim Alexander has opened up Fort Phantom to the public? Everybody is so proud of him. He's built roads, fenced it, and a few other things.

*   *   *

Spence: How are you this morning?

Jones: Oh, what a week last one was! You'll have to take care of writing history, because I'm spending my time on nervous breakdowns and falling arches, and a few other traumas. One day my car battery went dead on me. At the most inconvenient time, naturally. Then the heat went off in my house, and so I've been slowly freezing to death. Then Julia [Julia Pickard, her sister] walked into my house and there stood a burglar with my best jewelry—I'm bragging—sacked in a pillow case. He dropped it and ran from the house, but I haven't slept real well since. Will just have to go on living with it, I guess. I don't want to move.

Then Katharyn Duff's illness took us all for a shock. Mickey [Haynie] and I had dinner with her and Beth [Duff] last Monday and she seems almost recovered—only a very slight hesitation in hunting the right word. I don't think it would be noticed if we didn't know her so well.

I'll save up the other traumas and tell you about them some other time. Now, aren't you sorry you asked how I was?

Spence: I asked for it. Maybe it's time for the tide to turn and you'll be blessed with a long period of good luck.

Jones: I'll let you know.

Spence: Since we haven't met for some time, let's start right off with some hard work.

Jones: Let's go!

Spence: Starting then within the Legett household: Who was responsible in those early days for the Legett family's laundry?

Jones: Anybody. And I mean just anybody we could dump it on. I guess we lost an army of household hired help because of our mountains of washing—*never* laundry. You know Mother and her mania for cleanliness.

Spence: But there were times—between the hired help—when the Legetts had to do the washing themselves.

Jones: It makes me tired to think about it even now. Sometimes we all had to pitch in. I can remember the big black pot a-boiling in the back yard. Judge would fill the pot with water and build the first fire—we young'uns had to keep it going after that. We also had to chunk the clothes down under the boiling water every few minutes. With a broom handle. Then Mother, bless her, had to do the wringing and rinsing and hanging up. Maybe she didn't hate it as much as the rest of us did, because, now that I think about it, she also made the lye soap. Oh, that woman had energy to spare.

Spence: You indicated earlier that Lora was a good cook. What comes to mind first about her cooking?

Jones: I remember Mother baking for days before Christmas; coconut, caramel, and fruit cakes, cookies, and so forth. I can't imagine a present day household eating that much sweet stuff. Eating habits have certainly changed through the years.

Spence: Let's shift to the Legett children . . .

Jones: Uncle Sam sometimes called us the three-legged children . . .

Spence: O.K., let's talk about the three legged children: I suppose there were times when you all managed to embarrass Lora in public—especially during those days of nineteenth century Victorian morality.

Jones: If that's an accusation, I . . . we plead guilty. But Kade always started everything, I got blamed, and Julia did the crying. One day, when we were still quite little, Mother was bathing us—for the umpteenth time that day, I imagine—and there was a knock at the door. No one else was around so Mother had to answer it. Well, Kade, Julia, and I took this glorious opportunity to run out and climb the big umbrella tree just outside the kitchen door. We thought its heavy foliage would hide us and I guess it did. But Mother probably followed our wet trail to the tree. She called, but we pretended we weren't up there. So who should come climbing up that tree after us but the *preacher!* He was the one who had come to the door. There we sat, naked as jaybirds. Judge said Mother blushed all the rest of her life when that incident was mentioned.

Spence: Did Lora like to buy fashionable clothes for her children and for herself?

Jones: Mother was always quite stylish-looking, to me at least, "pretty as a picture" every time she stepped out. She saw to it that Judge was always proud of her. But I don't think she bought a great many clothes. She had that knack of accessorizing different costumes so that they looked different. I remember she wore a lot of gray.

As I remember our clothes [Julia's and Ruth's], Mother liked to dress us alike. Julia was a year and a half older, you must remember. Well, Mother would buy what looked good on Julia—and then get me one. We were entirely different, but I looked like exactly what I was: *Little Sister*. But I was twice as *big* as Julia and looked ridiculous. Which I knew. I am sure by the time Mother got to dressing me she was glad to have me covered. Julia was little and cute and looked darling in everything, and I just didn't fit the ribbons and bows at all. I could tolerate sashes but never ribbons and bows.

Spence: Given a full day at home alone, and all the regular chores done, Mr. Lamkin in control of the garden, and the

house sparkling clean, what do you think Lora was likely to do?
Jones: That kind of day never happened once, that I know of, but, here goes: She'd probably go trim the grape arbor, or prune the roses, or plant rose cuttings. All those things done, she'd go back and clean the house again. Then, she might sit down and read a new book. But in the daytime? I can't imagine it at all.
Spence: Let me rephrase the question: If Lora were *sitting down*, but not working, what would she be likely to do?
Jones: I'm stumped again. I can hardly remember her sitting down. But when she did, I can only think she was at some public place listening to somebody's speech or music or she would be traveling somewhere. Oh, yes, one other thing: she could indeed sit for hours—well, for an hour—to watch the sun set. Often she did that, wherever she was.
Spence: Your family took long and frequent trips around the country during your childhood. This was not common to the average frontier family, but was it typical of the more affluent Abilenians?
Jones: Mother was the reason we went on so many trips. She thought them up, Judge protesting all the time that we couldn't afford it. But, then, when we got back, he would tell at great length about the "fine, educational trip" he had just taken the family on. Mother enjoyed them herself, but I am sure she was determined, also, that we young'uns were going to know as much, and have been as many places, as other children.

I don't know if we were typical or not. Uncle John [State Senator Bryan] and his family went quite a few places.
Spence: I'm sure the readers of *Judge Legett of Abilene* are going to like my story of the rabbit funeral you and Kade and Julia conducted as children. Would you recount it now, and I'll include your version in *Trilogy?*
Jones: It was Julia's story, really. She tells it best, and she was also in charge of the "arrangements" so to speak. Julia, you see, liked more lady-like games, but Kade and I always wanted to go more rough and tumble: bronco bustin', climbing trees, that sort of thing. You know, I'm not sure I ever thought of it

before, but Julia must have thought at that age that she had two brothers instead of a brother and a sister.

Well, as I told you, we had a Belgian hare and it died. Julia was particularly fond of the poor thing and nothing would do but that we have a funeral for it, so—as Julia explained to Kade and me—it would go up to heaven. We must have fallen for that line, because next thing we knew Julia was in charge of the whole thing. Somehow she got me to give up my favorite little box I had treasured for years, so we could use it as the rabbit's casket. Kade didn't own anything clean enough or nice enough that Julia wanted to bury with the casket. Julia gave something . . . oh, yes, a really beautiful embroidered handkerchief—I can still picture it as she spread it over that poor little rabbit.

Only Kade could be the preacher. How I wish I could remember what he said! When it came time for a hymn, we all knew many a tune, but we hadn't paid enough attention in church to the words, so we knew no lyrics to any hymn. Finally, Julia, as the choir director—who else?—came up with "My Country 'Tis of Thee" which, I suppose, we had all been forced to memorize in school.

Well, all of this entertained us for an hour or so. After a few days, however, I was awfully sorry I had let Julia con me out of that nice little tin box. It was the only thing I could keep my precious jewels in, you see, my pirate's cache. One day she caught me red-handed: right in the middle of digging up the Belgian hare. She was shocked and outraged and ready to shoot me dead. But nothing for that: I kept digging. You know the end of the story: when I opened that box I closed it again real quick. I believe I smelled that thing for a week although Julia made me bury everything all over again.

Spence: Well, the clock says you have another appointment, so you won't have to confess any more sins today.

Jones: Saved by the bell. I keep thinking of these silly things in the middle of the night and promise myself I won't tell you, but I do every time. I'm just a ham I guess.

And by the way, we're all proud of you for having your Legett manuscript accepted by Texas A&M Press.

* * *

Spence: How are you this cold frosty morning?
Jones: I am about to feel human again after this two or three weeks' flu. Never was so very sick, but never *felt* worse mentally or physically. When I get like this I hate me, but don't want to go off and cut my throat. Mother would show up and then I'd have to clean up the mess.

While I was sick I decided to read my copy of the *Judge Legett* manuscript again—for the umpteenth time—now that Texas A&M Press has decided to publish it. I hope they're not making you cut too much out. Don't dare let them talk you into cutting out that part about Simmons College conducting a Bible Institute which often lasted for a week or ten days. I jotted down part of the program and that part which described the local accommodations for out-of-town visitors in January 1905. It goes something like this: *Board at private homes, Simmons College, and at some of the hotels will be $5 for the ten days term. There will be reduced rates at the wagon yard for teams . . .*

I think this wagon yard touch is superb. Could it be brought out more noticeably? I love it! I don't believe very many readers would realize there were wagon yards in and around Simmons as recently as that. I guess that really isn't very recent is it? But I remember it so well!

And don't let them cut out that part where the audience at a Simmons College lecture broke into loud applause when a Yale professor—William Lyon Phelps—expressed his opinion that the three greatest books ever written were the *Bible*, Bunyan's *Pilgrim's Progress*, and the works of William Shakespeare.

And I hope you'll keep that paragraph about the hen whose owner claimed she had laid 314 eggs in 365 days. Do you know why she missed fifty-one days that year?
Spence: No. But I have a feeling you do.
Jones: Why certainly: That poor hen wouldn't dare lay an egg in Abilene on Sunday!
Spence: I've got news for you: You have *fully* recovered from your recent flu.

Now, let's talk about Lora again. I also mention in the Legett book that Lora usually attended annual luncheons and business meetings for the Ladies Aid Society of the First Baptist Church. Do you have any recollections or comments to make on that?

Jones: Sure sounds dull. But heavenly, I guess.

Spence: Let me try another question: Other than the Ladies Aid Society, to what women's organizations did Lora belong?

Jones: The Twenty-One Club was quite a "prodder" in Mother's day. The Abilene Shakespearean Club. She was a charter member probably, and I think it was the first chapter in Texas. Nobody was *anybody* who didn't belong to that. But then there was an earth-shattering expose there one year, when it was found out that one of the pillars of the club had been "living in sin" with a man without benefit of clergy. Mother never recovered from that, and I'm not sure the town did either. I couldn't get Mother to tell me *who* never mind about *why*.

Spence: If we keep moving in this direction I'll have to ask *Playboy* magazine to publish *Trilogy* for us.

Now, another question: Your parents did entertain frequently in the Legett mansion?

Jones: Almost all the time. A stream of people would just "drop by," but they entertained a great deal, too.

Spence: Who were they?

Jones: It would be more accurate to say everybody than to try to list them. Church people, Simmons people, Judge's cronies, politicians, city hall people wanting Judge's opinion, clients, people in trouble in bankruptcy court. And then there were social friends.

Spence: What do you remember about Lora as a hostess?

Jones: She was a good one. Very, very organized and in control of things without too much fuss and bother—but always worrying about the acetylene tank just before the guests arrived.

Spence: This had to do with the lighting system before Judge Legett installed electric lights?

Jones: Yes. It seemed to Mother that the light would always go out just before the guests arrived for a big function, and one of us children would have to be on alert to run out in the yard and yank the lever that would dump some crystals down into the tank. This was supposed to happen automatically, and it would, except when the house was full of people. It was a beautiful kind of light, but sure not dependable.

Spence: When Lora Legett planned her open house at Christmas or New Year's whom did she ask to assist her?

Jones: Usually relatives and special friends. Poor Uncle Sam was always so stiff and unnatural-looking in Mother's receiving lines. Always in the house party was Mrs. A.M. Robertson, the social editor of the *Abilene Reporter*. Usually the door-opener. Otherwise, how else was she to know who was there?

Spence: Was Lora ever involved in Judge Legett's work for Simmons College or Texas A&M?

Jones: Mother was frequently at Simmons for social occasions. Teacher says he remembers her well as a "very gracious and charming woman" and I imagine she helped whenever the Ladies Aid Society was involved in something out there, but she rarely ever went to A&M with Judge . . . I started to say something I shouldn't, but I've promised myself I'll be good for the rest of the day. I'm sure when Mother did go to A&M with Judge, he was speaking or being recognized for something. But Julia and I weren't even allowed to *see* the campus. To this day neither of us has ever set foot on that campus. The way Judge saw it, an A&M college was no place for women. And yet, at home, we young'uns thought, barring Heaven, the Pearly Gates, and the Baptist Church, we would go to A&M when we died; probably preceded by Senator Joe Bailey [Joseph W. Bailey], Judge Meek [Edward R. Meek] and Lee Scarborough.

Spence: Would you ask Dr. Richardson, next time you see him, if he remembers any specific occasions when Lora was involved in Simmons activities?

Jones: Now how can I get any serious courting done if all I can tend to on my Saturday night dates is *your* business? But, yes, I'll ask him.

Spence: Was Lora likely to be in the audience when such celebrities as Jan Paderewski, Sarah Bernhardt, and Ida Tarbell came to Abilene?

Jones: Always. I don't recall any specific times, but she would go to any performance that had cultural merit. She and Judge frequently went to performances at the opera house.
Spence: Considering her limited opportunities to become involved in business affairs, Lora seemed quite informed on the Legett family's financial situation.
Jones: I've always thought so. Mother would economize and skimp and save endlessly to help Judge pay for new land, and I am sure she was the reason we had so many land holdings—I'm talking about those other than what she inherited. I really believe she was more accountable for Judge's purchases than he was. Judge readily said so.

Oh, I just thought of the perfect story to tell you to show how Mother would pinch pennies. It's been a family joke for years and years. Judge and Mr. Wagstaff went off on a business trip somewhere, from which Judge came back pretty exhausted. Mother suggested that he might be coming down with something, but Judge said no, he had just gone to bed later than he ever had before in his life. Mother wanted to know why. It was such a small town, you see, there couldn't have been anything to do. Well, Judge explained, he and Mr. Wagstaff had had to share a little room—maybe even the same bed—and neither of them was in any particular hurry to go to bed or even to undress. Each kept finding excuses to do something else before turning in. Finally, it just had to be faced: both of them were wearing homemade underdrawers made by their wives from old flour sacks. You see, Mother would do anything to save another dollar for more land, or for a trip or something more important than underdrawers.
Spence: A choice story. In my research I keep running into these flour sack drawers stories. I think this one deserves going into the *Trilogy*.

Well, our time is up again.
Jones: I don't know if we wrote any history, but its been fun.
Spence: If I may be my nosey self, again, what big plans do you have coming up?
Jones: Well, there's this TSHA business meeting here next

week. And, wouldn't you know, my yearly bridge tournament at the very same time. Guess which one will take all my time—the TSHA meeting of course. Teacher will have it no other way. I'll be lucky if I get to play bridge one time. I think I'll give a small cocktail party for about twenty at the Petroleum Club on Friday evening for some of Teacher's buddies: Joe Frantz—I love that man—Escal Duke, Kenneth Neighbors, Ann Brindley, Tuffly Ellis, and others. The Duffs and Ruth Gay will also be there. Now don't you wish you and Wanda [Mrs. Spence] would be in town, too?
Spence: Yes, indeed I do. Your parties are always the best.
Jones: Then, about a week later, Henry Doscher and I are taking Dr. Fane Downs from McMurry College to dinner. Hope your ears will burn. We'll certainly be talking about the Legett book coming out.

* * *

Spence: Good morning.
Jones: Good morning. I've decided to turn all of Judge Legett's papers over to the Richardson Research Center [at Hardin-Simmons University] now that you are through with them. There will be a dedication later this year, maybe in September.
Spence: An excellent place for them. I don't expect the A&M Press to suggest any more alterations to the Legett manuscript. But I have my own copy of the Legett originals if I should need to refer to them.
    What have you been doing since we last talked?
Jones: We had a grand time in Galveston. Teacher and I went with Dr. and Mrs. Aston, and they took care of the old folks. There was a program on the railroads I went to and Ben Proctor of TCU came up afterwards to Teacher and me and talked about getting you to give a paper on Judge. Next fall I guess.
    I was so tired when I got to Galveston that I all but tumbled into bed. Dr. Aston tucked us all in. I slept good and woke up raring to go, but I couldn't find my room key. I looked in everything I had, but decided I'd just have to ask the room clerk

for another one. So I went out the door and, lo and behold, I had left the key on the outside all night. Just shows you, I can't get into trouble when I try.

West Texas Historical Association meets here on April 2nd and 3rd. I am trying to get up my nerve to give a slight cocktail party between sessions. Oh, me. You and Wanda come help me.

Spence: We know you don't need any help in giving a party.

Jones: Teacher and I are going to the Institute of Letters on April 20 at the Baker Hotel in Dallas, and then the Association of Social Sciences later that week. You see, culture takes longer for some people than for others.

Spence: Let's talk awhile about Lora and her husband: There seems to be no question in your mind that your parents had a good marriage?

Jones: None whatever. I have thought about it often. The keynote of their marriage, I think, was their mutual respect for each other, and the fact that all decisions concerning the children were from both of them, and no fooling. I have seen Mother blink back a tear or two when she thought Judge was making too harsh a decision, especially concerning Kade, but in front of us, she went right along.

Spence: Fine. Now another topic: When the automobile replaced the horse and buggy, was Lora Legett among the first women in Abilene to drive?

Jones: Heavens no! But it was more Judge's fault than Mother's. He thought for years that cars were just a fad and would soon go away. There are a lot of stories about his driving that I forgot to tell you about for his biography. But Julia and Mother couldn't drive worth a dern either. I was pretty good, or always thought I was.

Spence: I want to hear about Judge's problems, too, but let's go to Lora's driving problems first. What do you remember.

Jones: Let's see . . . oh, the picnic! . . . We had just gotten Mother's new car and she thought she knew all about driving it. The man who sold it to her—one of the Spaulding-Windmill men, there on South First Street, just across from the present T&P depot—had driven her home in the car. Well, we had this ranch out at Elmdale by this time—about five or six miles out of town—where we often went, Judge to see about cattle and things and the rest of us just to get out of town.

We had to carry our food because there was only a big old Majestic range—probably the one we used to have in my childhood—that burned . . . wood? Coal? I don't remember, isn't that strange? Anyway, it took us hours to get the big bully going, and then we were uneasy about going off and leaving the fire. You, of course, don't remember old time fireless cookers. Well, Mother prepared the noon dinner in the fireless cooker at home: baked hen, dressing, gravy, rolls, cranberries, sweet potatoes, and other goodies, all carefully packed. The fireless cooker had clips that fastened securely the lid on to the pan. Uncle Sam, the funny one, was in the back seat of Mother's new car, and he was given the job of holding the chicken upright so it wouldn't spill. Away we went.

Pretty soon we all got to telling Mother she sure was driving slow, to whip it up. We complained that we might as well have taken the horse and buggy. That was the ultimate insult in those days. Well, of course you can guess what happened: She took off over a smallish ditch, about eighteen inches deep, through a high bob-wire fence, and into a freshly plowed field. Mother's was an open car and bob-wire was flying every place, clods from the field were pelting us, headlights falling off, and so forth. Lesser things like cookies, cranberries, milk, were also going everywhere. When finally the plowed ground stopped us, we all tumbled out. Most of us were white and shaken, trembling and wide-eyed. All but Uncle Sam. He got out of the back seat, proudly holding the fireless cooker lid firmly clamped down and announced: "Damn-golly, I never spilled a drop."

For many years, whenever anybody fell, slipped, or had an accident, the first thing said was "I never spilled a drop."

Spence: Did Lora ever get another car?

Jones: Oh, my, yes! One time Mother decided she wanted a Cadillac, but Judge griped and griped about it costing too much. Naturally he bought it and then couldn't resist showing if off as "my machine." He never called them cars. Luckily, the day he put a car through the back end of our barn, he was driving, or trying to drive, a Ford model T. You might say he never learned to drive anything, including a horse and buggy.

God was just good to us that Mother or Judge or Julia didn't kill half the population of Abilene.

Spence: Tell me one of your favorite stories about Judge's driving.

Jones: Well, the last one is one of my favorites. This happened soon after Mother's death. She had a new car and he decided to keep it. With Judge, every time he drove a new car he had to learn to drive all over again. *Nothing* carried over from the old car. Kade and I suffered and slaved over him. It took days. Finally we decided he could drive by himself. Several weeks went by. Nobody killed. Not even a dent in the fender. We were all delighted. Then one day Kade asked the cop who usually stood on Judge's office corner how Judge was doing in his new car. The cop said, "Oh, just fine. One of us stands on this corner and watches for Judge Legett to leave his office, then we alert the others down the street. They stop all traffic along Judge's route until he gets out of the downtown area."

Judge never knew this and thought until the day he died that he had finally mastered the art of driving.

Spence: The change from horse and buggy to automobile obviously brought considerable trauma to the Legett household. Do you recall a similar impact upon other Abilene families of that era?

Jones: Everybody was frightened to death of the "machine," whether they admitted it or not. One funny story comes to mind concerning Uncle John's and Aunt Mattie's family. Aunt Mattie always had to beg Uncle John or one of her boys to drive her to town in their Stevens-Duryea. One day she decided she would not ask them at all, she would drive herself. Of course she didn't know how.

Well, they all gathered in the back yard to see her get started. Turned out she did fine circling the block, but she decided she'd better not venture downtown. Only then did it occur to her to wonder how to turn the blasted thing off. Suddenly she started honking and yelling for one of them to jump in and stop the engine, turn off the ignition, shoot it, or something. They all just laughed and wouldn't help. The devils made her drive that car around the block until she ran out of gas. I've often thought since: wouldn't it have been fun if she had made a run straight at them?

Spence: Don't I recall, from *Judge Legett of Abilene,* that Senator Bryan also had great difficulty learning to drive a car?

Jones: Oh, he was the worst. Even worse than Judge. Uncle John was supposed to be a good senator, but I don't think he ever got the hang of riding a horse, let along driving a car. He was out at the Hamlin ranch one time mending fences; suddenly, according to Uncle John's version, the horse reared up and threw him off. But a hired hand's version was that Uncle John just rode that poor horse right over a bluff, not noticing what he was doing. Anyway, there was wild excitement that Sunday on how to get Uncle John to the Abilene hospital. There weren't many roads, and no good ones, and autos weren't too plentiful, so finally Percy [Jones, Ruth's husband] sent, or took, an Abilene and Southern engine, with a caboose attached, to Hamlin. Uncle John was pretty badly injured. Almost died, I think.

For some reason, another car story just popped in my mind, which concerns Kade. Do you want to hear it?

Spence: I want to hear every one you can remember. Could Kade not drive very well either?

Jones: Kade had very little more mechanical sense than Judge. I was the only one in the family who could understand how a car worked. You're smiling, but I'm not kidding! Anyway, this story doesn't concern Kade's driving, but it was one of his favorite stories.

One year Kade decided to build up the blood lines in Judge's cattle, and he talked Judge into buying a very fine, quite expensive Hereford bull. Big as a barn it looked, but gentle as a kitten. Well, Hector—the bull—got out on the main road one day and decided to take issue with an old Ford coming down the road. I am sure Hector thought the Ford was moving in on his territory, so Hector got right in the middle of the road and wouldn't budge. The car stopped, but suddenly Hector puts his head down and goes after the Ford. Kids were knocked every whichaway, fenders dropped off, headlights came loose from their bailing wire. The women and kids were all screaming bloody murder.

Kade was beside himself with anxiety, worry, and visions of a huge damage suit. He ran over and tried to see if anybody was hurt, then helped patch up the car, and all the time trying to get the man to give him an idea of what the damages were. That is, after he found that nobody was hurt.

The man was very evasive, sort of shifty-eyed, and chewing tobacco ninety to nothing. He just would not tell Kade anything. Finally, Kade said he would have to know.

"Well," the man said to Kade, "you have been awful nice about this, and it really was an accident; not your fault. Would $5 be too much to get the car back in shape?" Needless to say, $5 suited Kade just fine.

Spence: That is a good story. Sounds like Hector made a good watchdog, too. Now, let's go back to your parents' relationship. Do you remember any major disagreements between them? I don't have household disagreements in mind, but a disagreement on some religious or social issue. Some basic disagreement?

Jones: I started to say no, but you have just reminded me of the Big Baptist Schism brought about when three prominent Abilene men "furnished their houses with saloon furniture," as the rumor stated it.

Should I tell it? Teacher will kill me. But it's true; it happened.

Spence: Let me hear it. It sounds pretty historic to me. Tell Dr. Richardson that "the devil made you do it."

Jones: Well, here goes . . . higgledy. The shot heard around the world was a mere airgun report compared to the news that three Abilene churchmen bought pool tables for their homes, after the town had just voted out public pool rooms. The wailing, rending of garments, casting out of devils, had nothing to compare in fury with the evil let loose in Abilene when those same tables were moved to the respective homes. The "other two" men were asked to resign from the Baptist church, and do Methodists get a chuckle when they now drive by the Radford Memorial Chapel, (at McMurry College, a Methodist institution) for the Radfords moved their affiliation rather promptly.

Not long ago Teacher wrote a history of the First Baptist Church here and he almost ignored the whole thing. Needless to say, I have needled him many times on the subject. I even dared to remind him that he criticizes quite openly any historian whose work doesn't stick to the facts. But he says this is "different" because there was so much loose gossip involved that it is just about impossible to separate fact from fiction. You see now why I lose every one of those intellectual set-tos with him.

Teacher says Judge wasn't asked to resign along with the "other two men" because there was a question of *dancing*, too. The Radfords and, apparently the Scarboroughs, had "dancing rooms" in their homes, along with the pool tables. I told him that the Legetts did, too, but we called it a front porch.

This is where Mother's and Judge's disagreement comes into the story. Judge sat down at his desk in the library and started writing his resignation anyway. Mother went in there and they sat up half the night arguing and talking. Mother finally talked him out of it, but it wasn't easy.

Later, Lee Scarborough always claimed that Judge was responsible for Lee's going into the ministry. He was quite well known and, I think, head of the Fort Worth Baptist Seminary for a long time. So, you see, the pool table in his home didn't ruin him after all.

Spence: Did Judge keep the pool table after tempers cooled?

Jones: Oh, yes, indeed. There were so many neighborhood boys around all the time Judge bought it for their enjoyment. I think there were about four Scarboroughs and about seven Sayleses in our neck of the woods.

Spence: Did you play pool at home?

Jones: I loved to play but played mostly by myself, because the boys that age wouldn't have been caught dead playing pool with a girl. It was much later, after I started playing a pretty good game, that they agreed to play with me and then only if they wouldn't get caught by one of the others.

Oh, I almost forgot something Teacher said not long ago: There was a visiting VIP to Abilene a few years back and it turned out that he loved to play pool. Well, his hosts looked all over town for a pool table. You guessed it; the only one they could find in all of Abilene was at the Hardin-Simmons recreation hall. Teacher chuckled and said, "How times have changed!" I don't think he'd really mind my telling all this. Times *have* changed.

Spence: We'll shift the subject again: Do you think Lora was a good mother-in-law?

Jones: Of course no woman on earth could have been good enough for Kade, but Mother was one of Annie Maude's favorites in the family, so Mother must have been nice to her. I think Mother really liked both sons-in-law. They always got along beautifully. Mother always made a point of taking the men's side. But I think they really loved her, too.

Spence: Was Lora a good daughter-in-law?

Jones: I don't know. Mother didn't have much time for being a daughter-in-law. I think she and Grandmother Legett were utterly and completely different. Grandmother Legett was easygoing, and slow-moving. I suspect Mother might have thought Grandmother Legett was a little lazy. Probably my imagination.

Spence: Was Grandmother Lora Legett a good baby-sitter with your children?

Jones: She was a devoted grandmother, but not much of a sitter.

Spence: Was Lora an active and energetic woman as she grew older?

Jones: Well, as you know, she never really grew old. She was only fifty-six when she died. But until she fell ill, she seemed never to slow down.

Spence: Was she ill for a very long time?

Jones: No. As with everything else she ever did, she went rather quickly. Early in the year—it was 1923, wasn't it?—she seemed to slow down and lose her enthusiasm for things. Judge took her up to Mineral Wells, but that didn't seem to help. He even talked her into going to some little clinic or something over at Putnam. Quite primitive as I recall. She didn't want to go, but Judge was getting so concerned about the change in her that she went. Only for a short time.

Finally, Judge and Mother went up to the Mayo Clinic in Rochester where she had a long and exhausting series of tests. One of the Mayo brothers helped in the tests. They finally confirmed what the Abilene doctors had been hinting at all the time: Mother had a terminal cancer. She seemed to give up after that. She was back home awhile and then she died in April. I've always believed April was her favorite month in the year, but I never heard her say that. I do know she could hardly wait to get outside and putter in her flower gardens every spring. She did *so* want to help make Abilene pretty.

RUTH LEGETT JONES (1892-1978)

PART THREE

The Legett Mansion

RUTH LEGETT JONES
(1892-1978)

Ruth Legett Jones was born in Abilene, Texas, December 28, 1892. She was the second daughter and youngest of three children born to Kirvin Kade and Lora Bryan Legett.

Ruth's father, a native of Arkansas, opened a law office in Buffalo Gap, Taylor County's only town in 1879. On his arrival there he owned the horse under him and a small saddlebag of personal possessions. In 1881 Legett moved to a designated townsite named Abilene along the Texas and Pacific rails. Four years later he married Lora Bryan, the eighteen-year-old daughter of Washington Carroll Bryan, a rancher, who had recently moved from East Texas. The three Legett children thus were among the first generation of native born Abilenians. Lora and K.K. Legett, in spite of their youth, developed a strong civic consciousness which soon placed them among the town's leading civic and social workers.

Ruth's father was involved in more occupations than the practice of law. With strong support and encouragement from his wife, Legett operated stock farms and ranch lands, experimented with diversified farming, and devoted whatever spare time he could find to founding and promoting Simmons College [Hardin-Simmons University]. Convinced that higher education was the life-blood of the nation, Legett later served on the board of directors at the Agricultural and Mechanical College of Texas for eight years, four of them as chairman.

Ruth and her older brother and sister, Kade and Julia, were thus the fortunate beneficiaries of a solid and secure family unit, the children of intelligent, devoted, and relatively affluent citizens of their frontier community. K.K. Legett's talent and popularity made him an ideal candidate for public office, but he decided early in life to resist such temptation, convinced that the rewards of political life were too uncertain to subject his family to the whims of election day decisions. His own impoverished childhood spurred his ambitions to provide his own family with the security he had lacked. Above all else, he wished for his family a life of stability, refinement and respect.

Both parents seemed unusually determined to protect their children from cultural provincialism or parochialism. Since they lived in a relatively rugged and isolated frontier community, they emphasized the educational value of travel. Even on business trips back East, Legett took Ruth or one of the other children with him. On such journeys Ruth remembered recording her observations and experiences and wrote long descriptive letters back home. On family trips, the Legetts visited such distant places as Colorado, California, and Vancouver, and in 1907 they attended the Jamestown Tercentenary Festival in Virginia. Thus Ruth had no opportunity to develop attitudes of narrow provincialism as she grew interested in the world beyond the boundaries of her home town.

On the other hand, Ruth never tried to shake herself free from the dust of her native West Texas. As a child she was comfortable and content in an environment in which her father and mother worked mightily to rid Abilene of its "wild West" image. They saw to it that all three children studied music, refusing to acknowledge the obvious fact that each of them was tone deaf. On one occasion they asked Ruth's piano teacher for a progress report; the teacher searched desperately for a complimentary response and finally replied: "Ruth no longer straddles the piano stool like a pony. Already she's learned to sit sidesaddle!"

Such efforts toward social refinement, and such pressures from a proud father, rarely inhibited Ruth. She was both tomboyish and fiercely competitive in every activity not related to music.

Ruth's parents believed firmly that after-school chores built character in children. It followed, therefore, that Ruth, Kade, and Julia had plenty of character-building assignments at home: they gathered eggs, picked up chips for the fire, "wiped the stairs down," (or "up" depending upon the direction they were headed when they heard their mother's voice), spaded the garden, picked and strung beans, shelled black-eyed peas, shucked corn, dug potatoes, picked berries, "chunked" (with a broom handle) the clothes under water in a boiling washpot, made lye soap, and dug up Johnson grass—the *second* most boring of all jobs. Ruth's most hated household chore, however, was churning.

When Ruth reached her early 'teen years, her parents built a new home on Meander Street which local newsmen thereafter referred to as the Legett "mansion." From the moment the house was completed, it became one of the leading social centers for Abilenians of all ages; there were lawn parties, musical recitals, choir practices, club meetings, dances, local and state political conferences, and college board meetings. Visiting church and secular scholars often found themselves trapped in the library at the Legett home to have their brains picked by their host, who had never had their opportunities for a formal education.

The Legett children grew up knowing they had no choice but to go on to college. Ruth was encouraged to attend an eastern school where she might study and simultaneously observe the mores of a different section of the country. She decided therefore to return to the state where her mother first attended college, enrolling at Randolph-Macon Women's College in Virginia. She returned to Texas after two years, and primarily to please her father, completed her bachelor's degree at Simmons College in 1913.

On Christmas Day, 1915, Ruth married Percy Jones, a young Welshman. Jones was a civil engineer who came to the United States as an employee of his bachelor-uncle, Morgan Jones, a prominent railroad builder and operator. Ruth and Percy Jones continued to reside in Abilene where they became the parents of three children: a son, Grenville Dodge (who died as a youth), and two daughters, Julia and Edith.

Through the years the Joneses accumulated ranch lands, railroad properties, and other holdings. The discovery of oil deposits on their lands made them one of the wealthiest families in West Texas. Ruth never permitted her great wealth to lull her into a secluded, inactive private life, although she would go to almost any length to avoid public attention. Even as a young woman she took an active interest in the welfare of others. When still in her twenties, for example, she undertook to finance and direct a home economics class for Abilene's black females, and she provided financial assistance to many young blacks—both male and female—who sought a higher education. She provided, also, the first funds for immunization against disease for Abilene's needy.

During World War II, Ruth was active in the Bundles for Britain program and the British War Relief Society. Unable to locate office space in Abilene for a local Red Cross chapter, she unintentionally attracted public attention to herself when a newsman discovered that she had, with the aid of a soldier's wife, cleaned and repaired a former chicken coop and converted it into a Red Cross office.

Through the forties, Ruth limited her activities to those of a housewife and mother, but the marriages of her daughters and then the untimely death of her husband forced major changes in her life. Though still primarily interested in her family, Ruth Jones spent the next quarter-century dedicated to two new interests: philanthropy and the study of history. She established the Dodge Jones Foundation (named to honor her deceased son) and through it she contributed to endless public and private causes: the operation and expansion of M.D. Anderson Hospital and Tumor Institute in Houston; Abilene's three colleges (Hardin-Simmons, McMurry, and Abilene Christian) and their library programs; the West Texas Rehabilitation Center; the Young Men's Christian Association; Hendrick Medical Center's heart research and burn treatment facilities, and the Hendrick Retirement Center.

Ruth Jones and her family originated and solely supported "The Bridge," a unique self-help program for Abilene's underprivileged. In statewide programs, she contributed generously to programs dedicated to the care of West Texas land and the use of its products, to brush control work, and to major programs at Texas Agricultural and Mechanical University and Texas Tech University. To Abilene's youth she gave tennis courts, public parks, and swimming pools.

During most of the remaining hours of her day, Ruth Jones pursued, along with her life-long friend, Rupert Norval Richardson, a vigorous search for the truths of history. Across the nation—but especially in the Southwest—they were very active members of numerous historical societies and they rarely failed to attend their annual conventions and business meetings. Both were members of the prestigious Philosophical Society of Texas, and Ruth served for a time as its vice president. For many years she regularly attended—with a half-dozen close friends following in her wake—history courses at the three local colleges.

Amidst her almost hectic daily routine, Ruth Jones managed to remain a very private person who steadfastly refused to permit her picture or her name to be printed in local newspapers. Virtually every philanthropy was anonymously given, and on one occasion she threatened to withdraw a gift of land when well-meaning city officials suggested naming the completed public park in honor of a member of her family.

In later life, as she grew increasingly interested in history, and as she began to see her family and herself in historical perspective, she was less wary of public notice. As a consequence, in 1977, she accepted a Doctor of Humanities degree from McMurry College. Embarrassed, ill at ease, but obviously pleased, Ruth Legett Jones stood before a large and appreciative audience and heard herself praised as "one who has always looked upon her resources as a means of helping others."

Among friends, Ruth Jones was warm, outgoing, humorous, witty, and delightfully droll. On serious subjects she rarely allowed the conversation to center upon herself. As she began to see her life and times as part of a larger historical picture, however, she could be coaxed into reminiscing about her early years as a child of the frontier, and by this approach the author drew from her these conversations.

CONVERSATIONS WITH RUTH LEGETT JONES
(Concerning her life in early-day Abilene)

Spence: Good Morning; I see you've been reading about Old Hickory.
Jones: Good morning to you. I loved reading Margaret L. Coit's little book about Andrew Jackson. I read one-third of it the first day and night. It is most interesting and uncluttered. Judge told lots of stories about him, but I didn't have gumption enough to listen. I sure like the smaller size of the book, too. I feel like I have a great hole in my stomach from trying to read Frank Vandiver's book on John J. Pershing. Each volume is over five hundred pages. Teacher gave it to me for Christmas and I am enjoying reading it, but I already have bursitis and fallen elbows and failing eyesight and am not through the first volume yet.

I also read recently a new book by William Curry Holden and J. Evetts Haley called *The Flamboyant Judge.* It's about Judge Hamilton of Amarillo and the running of those huge Amarillo ranches. It's Teacher's book, but he let me read it. I'll bet it is up for a Texas Institute of Letters Award later in the spring.
Spence: What else have you been doing lately?
Jones: I just got back from a Western History Association meeting. Maude King, Dr. Zambus, Teacher, and I went together. We discussed rare books most of the way there and back. Dr. Robert G. Athearn was there. He has picked up some weight, but not much. I saw him just to say hello. Dr. and Mrs. Ray Billington were at the head table with Teacher and me and Ben Proctor. How do you like that for tall cotton? 'Twas fun, but, oh, what a dust storm on the way back!
Spence: A&M Press has put *Judge Legett of Abilene* "to bed" as they say. So they can't be asking for any more changes, nor can I.
Jones: The only change I would make is to leave out all those footnotes. I *hate* footnotes. Looks like you could have said at the bottom of each chapter "Ruth Jones is responsible for most of

the family dates, ages, and names." Then, when in doubt, you could say, "She said it, I didn't." You know as well as I do that Teacher wouldn't agree. So don't quote me. You see, my mental span is so short that when I have to stop to read a footnote I forget where I was.

I still can't see why one has to stop in the midst of a nice anecdote to learn it was mentioned, say, in the *Abilene Reporter-News* or somewhere like on April umpteenth, 1905 or thereabout. Couldn't they all be put in the back and lumped in a few pages? Then I could ignore them if I wanted to.

Now don't let the Historian know I said this. He thinks he's got me convinced.

Spence: Why do I have this feeling you are trying to delay talking about Ruth Legett Jones?

Jones: Do we have to?

Spence: If we don't, why are we calling this project *Trilogy*?

Jones: We could fool 'em.

Spence: We'd both have to answer to Teacher . . . Do you wish Vernon Spence had never been born?

Jones: Could be, but as long as you are here, I'll try to make the best of it.

Spence: Let's begin with a few comparisons with Sophia and Lora, and then we'll move on to your early childhood.

What were the physical similarities between Sophia Bryan, Lora Legett, and Ruth Jones?

Jones: In general appearance we were not much alike. Julia was the one who looked a lot like Sophia. Mother and I didn't look like them, but we didn't look like each other either. All had blue eyes. Sophia about average height—about five feet four, I guess. Her hair was almost black and never had a gray hair to the day she died. All three had straight hair; my hair is heavier and brown instead of near-black. Lora had beautiful hands, and it always pleased me no end when somebody would tell me I had my mother's hands. You must remember, I didn't get a lot of compliments.

Spence: What were your physical differences?

Jones: I was a lot taller than either of them; bigger feet, bigger hands—and hated every inch of it. I literally grew up feeling like a freak. Uncle John didn't help my self-image any. I don't ever remember going into a room where he was that he didn't say: "Great Jehoshaphat! How much taller are you going to grow?" Well, I didn't know, but I could have died right there with the greatest pleasure.

Spence: As children, you and Kade seemed to gang up on Julia. Did Kade and Julia ever gang up on you?

Jones: Oh, yes, many a time, and I was the poorest sport in the world. I'm sure it was because I was jealous of Kade. As I said before, I idolized him. But whenever they really wanted to get my goat, all they had to do was tell me that I was adopted. The war was on! That never failed to make me feel very insecure and unwanted, which, I wasn't smart enough to figure out, is what they had in mind.

Spence: I mentioned in *Judge Legett of Abilene* that you, Kade, and Julia rode a donkey to school on Pine Street. I think the readers of *Trilogy* would enjoy reading your own version of that experience.

Jones: Kade didn't ride a donkey. He had a pony. Julia and I had to *share* a donkey. 'Tweren't no justice in those days to be sure. That donkey hated going to school worse than we did. We were late almost every day and nearly always in trouble over it. We could have walked to school in half the time. But going home . . . that was a different story. The donkey went so fast that Julia would slide back onto me and I'd fall off the donkey's rear end. When I fell and broke a collar bone that put an end to that. Finished. Kaput.

Spence: Do you have anything to add to your bronco-bustin' story, which also appears in the other book?

Jones: I think you told most of it. We had a small—not too small—shed in the cow lot where we would lead a calf down under the roof. We would take turns holding him in place while the other would slide lickety-split down the roof and onto the calf's back. Out would come the calf a-pitching! But did we hate having to take Julia on such ventures. She would always get hurt and go yelling to Mother, who would then come out and

say, "Now Ruth, you be nice to your little sister." Julia, remember, was a year and a half older than I was! The sissy.
Spence: I suppose the most popular story about yourself in *Judge Legett* concerned the day you stripped naked to swing across a small pond and got caught mid-stream by some neighborhood boys. Kade had convinced you that the pond was very deep, but, nevertheless, better to drown than be caught naked in front of a bunch of boys; so you released the rope and dropped into about three inches of muddy water. Do you recall any other details of that story?
Jones: I remember that two of the boys were brothers: Tom and Eugene Pearce. In those days of great modesty, I would have been better off dead. I remember my parents didn't love me much for some time thereafter.

I forgot to tell you awhile ago that donkey's name was Kirk. Which reminds me, you never did tell the name of that horse Judge first rode out to Buffalo Gap in 1879. Don't you know it? It's very important to know that horse's name.
Spence: I never did run across a reference to its name. Judge mentioned several times that it was a good horse but he never gave a name.
Jones: It couldn't have been an expensive horse in those days. Judge was too poor. Maybe he meant it was dependable. In those days it was unthinkable for a horse not to have a name.

Some of my earliest memories are of our beloved pets having rabies, going mad, and having to be destroyed. What heartaches those occasions were! I don't suppose we had ever heard of rabies serum. There was a "mad stone" that could sometimes be gotten and placed on the dog; where, I have no idea. I can't remember one ever doing any good. Some of our ranch animals—dogs it seems—had "happy rabies." Did you ever hear of that? Extremely exuberant, happy, jumping all over their loved ones. More difficult to detect than the frothing at the mouth, biting, type. Anyway, I've just gotten over being afraid of rabies. Or have I?

Teacher and I were talking one day about mad dogs and mad stones and he said he had the same fear of rabies as I did.

He said he had a mad stone given to him by his grandmother, probably from the Civil War days. I can't hardly imagine *me* being before rabies serum, but I sure was.

You know, somehow I want Judge's horse to have a name. I *know* it had one. I remember the names of lots of our horses, but I don't ever remember hearing that horse's name.

Spence: And if you had ever heard it, I don't doubt that you would still remember. Back to the Legett children: For how long did the Legett children study music?

Jones: We all dropped music at a very early age. I'm not even sure that we ever picked it up in the first place. Kade and Julia were worse than I was, if that is possible.

Spence: You have mentioned several times that Kade was your idol.

Jones: Yes, I really and truly did idolize him. I used to hide his report cards, at his request, to keep the family from knowing how bad his grades were. It is a good thing he didn't ask me to kill somebody, for I sure would have tried to.

Spence: I have here a line or two your father wrote to a sister on December 19, 1904: . . . *They have all been in school all their lives and all taking music, Kade on the cornet, Julia on the piano and violin, and Ruth on the piano. They play some. After a while we hope to have good music in our home . . . .*

Jones: That they never got. By anybody's standards we were awful. You notice that Judge said: They play *some."* Well, even that was an outrageous exaggeration.

Spence: You use the term "wiping down the stairs" as one of the childhood chores you despised. What did it involve?

Jones: I hardly ever remember going up or coming down the stairways without Mother being at the head or the foot with a rag which she would throw to me saying, "Wipe the stairs down." I used to try to fool her by going up the other, front or back, but she always caught me. And then the porches. They were endless. Miles of them across the front, upstairs and down, and then all the way across the south and west sides of the house. I am talking about the big house on Meander now. There was a wide cement walk from the house down to the street, also miles long, and Mother thought it had to be swept every day. Oh, me!

Spence: Since Judge Legett hated to churn more than any other household chore, and since the children also hated it more than anything else, I suspect Mrs. Legett did most of the churning.

Jones: What would make you think that because we children hated to do anything we didn't have to do it? We're talking about the days when the grownup folks were in charge . . . because they were bigger, I guess.

Spence: You seemed to be much closer to your Grandmother and Grandfather Bryan than to your Legett grandparents, even though you've said that your Grandmother Legett was a much better cook.

Jones: Yes, that's true. Grandmother Legett's big, old, fat biscuits with brown sugar on them were infinitely better than Granny Bryan's cold, yellow corn bread. I think Granny Bryan must have made that hated corn bread in hogshead barrels. She never ran out of it; probably because nobody ever ate it.

Spence: But you didn't often visit Grandmother Legett . . .

Jones: No, because they lived in Buffalo Gap while they were in West Texas, and it took awhile to get out there. They didn't live in West Texas at all during most of my childhood. They could never stay in one place long. Judge built their little Buffalo Gap house and gave it to them, but in a few years they left and went somewhere else.

Spence: So you don't remember much about their place in Buffalo Gap?

Jones: Not very much. I do remember a huge, old climbing-tree, a pecan or oak maybe, in their yard. Lots of big trees in Buffalo Gap, you understand. Well, as I guess I've made overly clear, I loved to climb, and so of course anytime we were at Grandmother Legett's I was in that big old tree. I should have told you in the beginning that, for some reason when I was a child, I was scared to death of a donkey's hee-haw. Not of the donkey, just his hee-haw. Kade insisted on calling them jackasses to Mother's frequent mortification. One day I got in the top-most branches of the big tree and the donkey—you guessed it—let forth with its best effort: heeeeeeee-haaaaaaaaw! I turned loose of any hold I had to anything and hit every branch on the way down. It scared me so bad maybe that is one reason I don't like high places, or flying, today. And that reminds me, Katharyn Duff promised to take me out to see what's left of that old house. It must look awful; she hasn't mentioned it since.

Spence: Our time is up again. But before I go, tell me what big items you have on your calendar for the next few weeks.

Jones: Well, for one thing, Buffalo Gap's one hundredth anniversary is this June and Katharyn Duff is already planning big things. I have promised to give the Historical Survey Committee a party on that date, and then the next day we'll all go to Albany to the Fandangle and to see Clifton Caldwell's new ranch house. I wish I could take the Historical Survey Committee to some fancy place to eat, say like a super-duper dinner at Tour d'Argent in Paris. That used to be the most interesting place and the food was divine. It's probably a "pot parlor" by now.

*   *   *

Spence: Good morning.

Jones: Good morning. If I don't write things down as they occur to me it's "goodnight Irene." So, if you'll ask me the right questions I might give you some answers. Didn't we have a lulu of a sandstorm yesterday? The worst one I have seen in years. First it rained, and then the sand came, and it looked like a huge mud pie, and my car was a knife slicing into it. Now look at it today: balmy and serene and looks like the weather is saying, "I never did anything like yesterday, ever!"

It's been so dead around here. The three D's—dead, dry, and dull—for sure. Nothing has happened. One man killed his wife or girlfriend or something, but, darn it, I had never heard of them before.

Spence: I have some spot-questions today, still about your childhood. Sort of a potpourri. First, you also list as one of your worst childhood chores digging up Johnson grass. Comment on that.

Jones: Anything I can tell you would be bad. The whole thing was always Mother's idea, being clean and neat as usual. Johnson grass was a terrible pest in gardens and field, not to mention the yards. Mother used to challenge us to see who could find the longest root, and then she'd give the winner a nickel or a penny or something equally impressive. Sometimes we would dig like crazy and build our riches by our side. There was a reward, also, for the highest pile of roots. Mother would then come out and appraise our work. Kade, the prize stinker, wouldn't work near as hard, but he always had the longest root or the highest pile. It took us years and years to figure out that he was swiping from our piles and claiming them.

Spence: Let's switch to something you enjoyed doing: What was your most frequent pastime at about age ten?

Jones: Trying to survive an older brother or sister. Trying to get a new dress that suited me instead of Julia—one that was not frilly, and was the right color.

Spence: O.K. Now, in another direction: Do you remember the first refrigerator in your home?

Jones: No, but I remember clearly our first ice box, the kind that opened from the top. The ice blocks were delivered by horse and van in 25, 50, and 100 pound blocks, depending on the color of the card Mother placed in the kitchen window. I remember when we'd chip off lumps for tea on a hot summer day. It was heavenly.

Spence: In the Legett book I described the interior of your home on Meander Street this way: *The first floor [included] a combination entrance-library-stairway (with extended platform), a "front room," a parlor, a dining room, a butler's pantry, a kitchen, and a master bedroom suite with separate bath and sitting room. The second floor included five bedrooms, a sun room (seldom-used sitting room), and a game room.* Does this bring to mind any additional descriptions or events associated with those rooms?

Jones: I remember a little Dallas News stove for quick heating in the sitting room of Mother's and Judge's bedroom suite. We young'uns, on cold mornings, would all run down from our

bedrooms upstairs, clothes in hand, to dress. I think there were seven fireplaces, too, three upstairs and four downstairs. I've already described the cooking stove: a fine, big majestic range, burned wood and maybe coal, had a huge hot-water heater on the back. Always something good-smelling on the stove.
Spence: Apparently there was a constant parade of visitors into the Legett home throughout your childhood.
Jones: A *parade* is exactly the right word; and sometimes a circus parade.
Spence: Do you remember any special ones?
Jones: Senator Joe [Joseph W.] Bailey comes to mind immediately. Judge almost revered him. I think it was mutual. He was a guest in our house many times—every time he was in Abilene. Had some member of the Heavenly Planet been there he wouldn't have been treated with more awe by us children. We were brought up yelling "Hoorah for Joe Bailey" often and loud. After the Waters-Pierce Oil Company scandal—which some people accused Senator Bailey of being connected with—I can remember Judge and Mother whispering to themselves about it. They would hush when we came into the room. I was in college before I ever learned what had happened.
Spence: Who else was a memorable house guest?
Jones: Gee, I don't know. One of my favorite couples lived right here in Abilene, but they were at our home often: Dr. and Mrs. J.T. Harrington. Judge was a good friend also of his brother, Dr. H.H. Harrington, who was president of Texas A&M when Judge was on the board down there. But Dr. and Mrs. J.T. Harrington were a delight. Dr. Harrington was slightly cross-eyed, a real tiny little man that we all adored. Mrs. Harrington was the Zazu Pitts type, also delightful. They later moved to Waco, so I guess they were staying with us the time Dr. Harrington came into the house, threw up his arms to hug Judge, and knocked off the glass shade on the overhead ceiling light in the entranceway. It fell, crashing, over Mrs. Harrington's head. She was busy talking to Mother. All she said was, "Oh, dear," brushed off the broken glass and kept right on talking as if that kind of thing happened to her every day. They were both priceless. I think Dr.

Harrington delivered all three of the Legett children. Maybe I'll remember some others later. There were so many they seem just a blur now.

Spence: Fine. You said you spent your early childhood surviving your older brother and sister, so now tell me what was your favorite pastime at about age fifteen?

Jones: Riding my favorite pony Nell all day every day. It seems like that's about all I ever did at that age.

Spence: You have also said, or suggested, that Kade was accident prone.

Jones: Yes, But it would take years to tell about all of his accidents. The only times he wasn't out looking for new ways to break his bones was when he was sick in bed.

One time he had enrolled at the University of Texas. He had finally decided he really did want to get an education. Said he had fooled around long enough. So he went to Austin. He seemed to be doing very well, at last, when he took typhoid fever. He came within an inch of not recovering. Couldn't continue in school of course. They had to bring him home on a stretcher after weeks in the hospital down there.

Then there was the summer Kade was visiting in Ann Arbor, Michigan. He went swimming in a swimming hole out in the country, dived into the water, hit a huge jagged rock just under the surface, and cut his head open fairly badly. Very nearly lost his life.

Before that, Kade rode out to the pasture one Sunday afternoon to bring in the horses. Somehow a very gentle and old gray mare kicked him right off the horse he was riding. He had a badly broken leg, was in bed for a long time. It was a typical disaster: before he could get around again they had to rebreak the leg and set it again.

Then there was the time he had just an ordinary—for other people—tonsillectomy and came near bleeding to death on two different occasions. The young doctor in town who finally stopped the bleeding literally put his thumbs in Kade's throat and pressed the bleeding parts until they quit.

Oh, Kade was trying to konk out all the time...but enough.

Spence: Let's shift to a pleasanter subject: What do you remember about the family's first trip to California and the tour of the Northwest?

Jones: I remember most of that first trip. For some reason that trip made an indelible impression I will never forget. The details are clearer than our later trips.

It was Mother's idea from the outset, but Judge, typically, took entire credit for it. The night before we left on the train, Mother put down pallets and quilts on the south porch for us to sleep on, because she didn't want to leave the house in disorder, beds unmade, and so forth. The train came through Abilene sometime in the middle of the night and somebody drove us to the depot in the surrey: Judge, Mother, Kade, Julia, me, our grips, valises, and all the things a family of that size would need for most of the summer. How do you suppose all of it got into one conveyance?

Mother, Julia, and I slept in one berth and Judge and Kade in another. Don't you know we had a restful night? I remember Mother and Julia got pretty put out with me because I kept sitting up to look out the window.

Spence: Well, then, let's call it a day. I'm sure you have a project of some sort underway.

Jones: Sort of. Pete Couch and I are seeing Teacher in about one hour and taking him my microfiche that Pete gave to me last year. Pete is letting me turn it over to the Richardson Research Center. Teacher has actually drooled over it ever since I got it. Worthy Long seems to be in on the project, too. No photographers...just us. I am bracing myself already for Worthy's usual greeting: "Look at that big hunk of marvelous womanhood!" He hasn't said it yet that I haven't turned around and looked behind me.

Then, Henry Doscher gets his master's in history from Hardin-Simmons on Sunday and is giving a party. All the history department at Simmons will be there. Everybody I know is making a dip and taking it to Henry's house—which is cute, but about as big as one of my larger closets. But it's always fun over at Henry's. He got a master's in history just because he likes history, I guess. Maybe it will help him in law somehow. I think he just likes to go to school.

You know, I have been badgering Teacher for years to start thinking about a joint PhD program for the Abilene colleges. I don't mean to say that Teacher opposes it, but I have certainly camped on his trail about it ever since I first started back to school. I still can't see why it wouldn't work. I even got him to say he would mention it to you sometime. I guess he will write to you himself. I hope he will, because I do prefer him to speak his own mind...imagine it being otherwise!

* * *

Jones: Hi! I can tell just by looking at you that you've got hundreds of questions that I can't answer.
Spence: Why don't you do all the talking, then I'll not have a chance to ask nosey questions.
Jones: Well, I do have a little story to tell that I think you'll enjoy: Our friend Joe Frantz (University of Texas history professor) wrote to me and told me that the TSHA is giving Teacher its first Leadership Award. (The award was established with funds provided by the Texas Education Association of Fort Worth, a private foundation, which encourages support of consitutional government through educational media.) Dr. Frantz wanted to know if I have a suitable picture of Teacher which could be provided to newspapers carrying the story. He said the award is not to be announced until the final day of the meeting of the Association this year, and Dr. Frantz was hesitant to request a picture from the Hardin-Simmons publicity department for fear somebody might let the cat out of the bag.

He ended his letter with "Yours in sin and conspiracy." Well, I found a picture and sent it to him with my little note attached: "Here's the conspiracy. I'll take care of the sin when I get to Galveston."
Spence: Well, then, maybe you shouldn't go to Galveston.

Jones: Honey, I've looked there before. There is no sin in Galveston.
Spence: You mean to say it's all just *talk?*
Jones: Every bit of it. But I'll look again.
Spence: What else have you been plotting and planning lately?
Jones: I'm not through telling you where I've been yet.

I was in Austin last week picking up more culture. And then Teacher and I went to a meeting of the Texas Institute of Letters in Houston. It was super. It is always one of my favorite meetings...

Something just popped in my mind that I don't think I ever remembered to tell you. It must have been three or four years ago. I think it was at a THSA meeting in Austin. We were headquartered at partially finished Driskill Hotel. Loads of people were coming by to comment on your first book (*Colonel Morgan Jones*). No, I can't remember any of their names, except this one named Dunnigan, I think. We were walking together to a session on railroads and he said he had just finished a book on a railroad man that was most interesting. You guessed it: *Colonel Morgan Jones.* Since you weren't there, I took the bow for you.

As I said, the Driskill was being remodeled at the time. It is dear to everybody in Texas.

I've rattled on long enough. What are we going to talk about today?
Spence: You haven't said much yet about the family trip to the Jamestown Tercentennial Exposition in 1907. What do you remember about it?
Jones: Quite a bit, but not very much that's historical. You see, I was thirteen years old and Julia fifteen. We didn't appreciate the historical nature of the trip at that time.

Kade was at Culver Military Academy in Indiana and he and quite a few of his corps friends came to Norfolk, Virginia, while we were there. Gee! they were pretty boys. Julia was impressed, too, and she should have been since they paid so much attention to her. In fact she got so excited she spilled a glass of ice tea in her lap and on her best dress. Mrs. Culver was there as a chaperon to the boys, and she helped Mother dry Julia's dress.

You see, my mind was not too much on Jamestown. Blame it on my age.

Oh, I just remembered another Abilene boy in the Culver Military Academy group that met us in Norfolk: Moliere Scarborough. We called him Moly. And another one! Seth Sayles was there. My, the things you are causing me to remember. Now, if I could only remember something about Jamestown.

Spence: Maybe we can come back to it again. Before the automobile came to Abilene, what kind of transportation vehicles did you have around the Legett house?

Jones: We had two or three buggies always, a surrey with fringe on top for the family, and a lighter buggy that Judge would drive us kids to school in.

I never saw Mother harness a horse or saddle one, and, if I remembered right, Julia harnessed a horse just once—to my sorrow. Somehow I was always elected when Judge or Kade weren't around, which was quite often. One day Julia wanted me to go to town with her. I said I'd go only if she would harness the horse. Well, she did and away we went. We got right down to town, in front of the drug store where all the boys hung out—I was driving of course—and all of a sudden I had to stop the horse *fast*. I've forgotten why. Anyway, when I stopped the horse the shafts flew up over his head. The belt around his middle hadn't been well-fastenend, and the belt, crupper and all, fell off on the ground. And there we were in our best dresses primly on our way to the drug store for a limeade.

Well, you-know-who had to get out, raise the horse's tail, put the crupper under it, fasten the belt, calm the horse, and so on. Julia helped by weeping some very becoming tears, although she didn't smear her powder one bit. I don't know if we ever got to the drug store that day, but I do know it was the only time Julia was ever allowed to harness the horse.

Spence: How did the coming of the automobile to Abilene affect 'teen-agers such as you and Kade and Julia?

Jones: In many ways; not all good either.

Spence: What do you have in mind?

Jones: Your question makes me think of Uncle John's and Aunt Mattie's two boys—our cousins—Bernard and Juel Bryan. Julia and I adored the Bryan boys and would run off and go anywhere with them. Judge and Mother thought they were sort of wild and reckless; now where do you think they ever got that notion? All we ever did was race the T&P passenger train every afternoon from Abilene to Merkel or Tye. The engineer and fireman got to know us real well. We would honk and they would toot back. The Bryans had a Stevens-Duryea, which was supposed to be something special.

We would race the train to see who could get to this particular crossing first. One day it was almost a tie, and we were going too fast to stop, but not fast enough to get across. Off the road we went, bouncing down the cotton rows and holding on for dear life. The engineer tooted at us and the last thing we saw was a puff of black smoke, compliments of the fireman.

Spence: Did Judge and Mrs. Legett ever hear about this?

Jones: No! We'd lie like old Billy when we were asked where we'd been. You see, that was the trouble with parents in those days, they never seemed to understand anything like cars and trains racing across the prairie.

I *never* told the truth, it seems like, while I was growing up. I could never see any good reason to risk a licking when by a well-placed fib I could avoid it. But I could never figure out how Judge and Mother could tell when I was telling the truth or not. When I figured that out I quit fibbing . . . and if you'll believe that you'll believe anything.

Spence: According to Ruth Jones, Ruth Jones was the only person in her family who knew anything about automobiles.

Jones: But *that's* the truth! I believe I could yet make a fair living on greasing old-timey cars that had grease cups. You had to unscrew, empty, clean out old grease, refill, and replace. The locations were in the most impossible places. Judge always said it took a contortionist, not a mechanic, to fix a car. But I loved it.

Spence: Who taught you how to do all of that?

Jones: Eddie Rickenbacker.

Spence: The First World War ace?

Jones: Who else?

Spence: Are you fibbing again?

Jones: No, no. Rickenbacker came to Abilene to give driving lessons. I think Ross Hall, who was selling Reos or maybe Firestones, sponsored him. He wasn't famous then, you understand. That was before the war.

Spence: Let's talk now about Judge Legett for awhile. It seems to me that he had one custom with his children that was most uncommon for fathers of his day: from your earliest years he regularly took one of the children with him on business trips. Your sister Julia once told me about one of her earliest recollections as a child: Judge and one of his business associates in Austin trying to figure out which was the front and which was the back of her dress. This would suggest that he was available at other times to act as chaperon, maybe during your 'teen years.

Jones: Yes, he was. I really believe Mother convinced him of the educational value of travel and I generally gave her the credit for our cross country trips, but Judge was also unusual in that way. I probably never gave him the proper credit.

I remember one trip to Dallas when he acted as a chaperon. Fay Young [Trammell], a cousin of ours, and Julia, and I wanted to go to the state fair at Dallas, and for some reason, I don't remember what it was, Mother wasn't able to go with us. Maybe Judge was going to Dallas anyway on a business trip. Anyway, off we went: three silly girls and Judge. Fay was some years older than Julia and I. Well, we were staying at the Oriental Hotel—it's the Baker Hotel now—and we finally got Judge on the street car and headed off to the fair grounds, planning to stay all day.

Just the instant the street car began to move, Fay dramatically clutches her bosom and literally screams—like only silly 'teen-agers can do—"I've left my diamonds at the hotel!" Well, Judge quickly decides that he'll get off and walk back to the hotel, locate Fay's rings, and join us later at the fair.

The hours flew by and we really forgot that Judge was in the world. When, finally, our legs, our feet, our money gave out, we hastened contritely back to the hotel, wondering all the while why Judge never had joined us. We rushed up to our suite to find Judge sitting calmly in a comfortable chair in the middle of the room completely encircled by what looked like every newspaper published in the United States that day. There was a mountain of them. He explained that he had looked for just a few seconds in our bedroom for the rings, but that we had left everything in our room in such a shamble that "a cow couldn't find her own calf in there." So, instead of wasting his time looking, he decided to stand guard over the rings so nobody else could steal them. That was Judge: imperturbable always.

Spence: I found among Judge Legett's papers numerous newspaper clippings on various topics. Several of them concerned proper behavior for young men and young women. I have one of them here with me. It states: *Girls, it's allright for you to have a "fellow" and go here and there with him, but don't be everybody's girl just because he asks you to be . . .*

Jones: Shucks, Judge didn't have to worry about that; they never asked me to be.

Spence: Here's another old newspaper clipping. This is by Mrs. A.M. Robertson, the society editor of the *Abilene Reporter-News*. She describes the Legett home at Christmastime: *The reception hall, corridors, and parlor are exquisitely decorated with all kinds of greenery, red berries, and New Year's bells, while in the dining room garlands of greenery, showered with sweet peas, are draped from the ceiling to the four corners of the room. The table is laid with cluny lace on which rests cut glass vases filled with red carnations. Crystal sticks hold crimson tapers with red sashes. Cut glass compotes hold red and white mints.* Do you remember these details?

Jones: As if it were yesterday. That would be the Christmas before my eighteenth birthday [December 28]. You must understand that Mrs. Robertson had a way with words—full of adjectives and adverbs and things—but yes, that description, as I remember it, is quite accurate.

Spence: You have indicated that Thanksgiving Day was also a particularly festive holiday in the Legett household. Let me quote a brief passage from *Judge Legett of Abilene* to refresh your memory: *Festivities began on the morning of Thanksgiving Day after the family attended special church services at the First Baptist Church and gained momentum during the holiday dinner when the John Bryans, the Sam Youngs, the Walter Trammells joined the Legetts. Festivities continued through the following week-end as male members—and some of the females—spent the remainder of the week-end hunting quail and dove in the hill country of south Taylor County or in the shinnery of Jones County.*

Jones: Yes, that's true enough, except that we would go out to the Elmdale ranch, too.

Spence: I also mention in the Legett book the difficulty of locating a Christmas tree tall enough to satisfy your mother. Can you add to what you have already told us about that?

Jones: I remember we almost burned down the house one year. You left that out of the book.

Spence: I don't think I've heard that story.

Jones: I must have forgotten to tell you. There was no such thing as a string of electric lights, so we had tiny candles that were in little tin holders that clamped on the limbs of the tree. Each one had to be individually lighted, but they were very effective. At one Christmas party—I think we were all 'teen-agers and dating—there must have been forty young men and women there. We had Frank Weaver, Yager shoe store owner, dressed as Santa Claus. He was to give out the presents. We all assembled in the parlor. When the candles were all lighted, the huge sliding doors were rolled back and the tree and room did look lovely. The rest of the house was dimmed or dark and the tree was a beautiful sight.

Santa—Frank—leaned down, picked up one of the presents and turned to Laura Batjer Jennings and said, "Here is a gift for little Laura." At that moment the tree caught fire and it blazed like a wild fire. Strings of cranberries and presents went up like fury. All the girls started screaming and some of the boys grabbed the tree and dragged it outside, still blazing.

Spence: You had no touble remembering that Christmas. Do you recall others?

Jones: No particular one. When we moved to the big house we hung our stockings over the mantel in Judge and Mother's bedroom on the first floor. No central heating, of course, so we would fly down to their room in our shimmy shirts at daybreak to see what we had in our stockings.
[NOTE: At this point the conversation was unexpectedly interrupted.]

* * *

LETTER: JONES TO SPENCE, APRIL 4, 1977

Things are happening so fast here I hardly know where to begin. First, Dr. Skiles [President, Hardin-Simmons University] is back in town and when he hears of all the doings he immediately says to Teacher, "That autograph party [for Judge Legett of Abilene: A Texas Frontier Profile] belongs to HSU. We want the whole thing, invitations, food, flowers, etc." Teacher hastened to assure me that he had not intimated such a thing, and I believe him. I am thrilled to death, and slept better than I have in a couple of weeks. The fact that Dr. Skiles asked for it pleased us all. I am now waiting for a return call from Mr. Wardlaw [Director, Texas A & M Press]. He is just back from a vacation in Carolina. I'll finish this letter after I've talked to him.

(Tuesday a.m.) Mr. Wardlaw plans to be here, and his wife if humanly possible.

Dr. Skiles has been most cooperative and accommodating. A love, in fact. He seems as interested in the autograph party as Katharyn Duff, or Dorothy Stowe, or me or anybody. Katharyn says Dr. Skiles has appointed dozens of people on committees, even called the Reserves about parking cars. They've decided to use the full first floor of the library. I had planned to have Zachary make some very nice invitations but cancelled when HSU took over. Dr. Skiles immediately brought Zachary back into the picture. He asked if 2000 invitations would be enough. I nearly fainted—Teacher says maybe one-tenth of that number might come if its a pretty day.

I am trying to break in new shoes so my feet won't hurt me at the party. I know after a couple of hours on my feet they'll hurt something awful, to say nothing of my facial musles from smiling all that time.
   See you.

* * *

Spence: Good morning. It's good to know that you, too, survived the autograph party.
Jones: Wasn't that something! I had no idea it would turn out to be such a huge affair. Teacher didn't either. I was exhausted, but wasn't it fun?
Spence: Except for the heat. I just wasn't expecting 88-degree weather on November 20. I should have known better than to bring from Virginia only mid-winter clothing.
Jones: You are a mess. Teacher says your second book is good, and so do I. We still laugh to each other about our efforts to get you to write or talk Texan. The expression I think is the most "down East" was about Mother "inspecting our clothing" for evidence of forbidden slides down the roof of the barn. I think I told you that she had us to bend over so she could look at "the seats of our britches." Same thing but different, isn't it?
Spence: Yes, but your expression is much better than mine.
   What have you been doing since the autograph party?
Jones: I loved reading the book [William W. Warner, *Beautiful Swimmers*] that you gave me, but now that I am an expert on the sex life of a Chesapeake Bay blue crab, where am I going to be able to use all this information? I could hardly put it down. Now you know that blue crabs aren't all that interesting, but that book was. I feel like I know several of those big Jimmies well enough to give them names. The author made them sound like real live people and I fell completely in love with the boat Little Doll.
Spence: Let's get back to our own book. Would you like to talk about the Elmdale ranch?
Jones: Suits me. What do you want to know?

Spence: You often mention the Elmdale ranch and the ranch house, but I don't have a very clear picture of it. Tell me about it—who operated it, how often were you there, why were you there, and so forth.

Jones: It was a smallish ranch—just 1250 acres—a few miles east of Abilene, and convenient because we could get out there in less than an hour even in the surrey. Less than that in the car—if it didn't break down or go in a ditch.

Judge raised commercial grade cattle there. He had a Negro foreman; Kade more or less took over in later years. They farmed a little bit of it. Mostly grain. I guess to try to make the raising of cattle less expensive. There were trees along the draws that followed the little creek that ran through the ranch. The creek—Rainey, I believe—was dammed up right in front of the ranch house and there was a lovely little lake there. An excellent swimming hole, until Kade's wife, Annie Maude, and two beautiful little girls were drowned there one awful day.

Our ranch house there wasn't used much for entertaining. That vogue hadn't come in then. But the family week-ended there a lot. Wood stoves, no help, groceries hauled from town, ice also. It was cooler out there. That's probably why we were going when Mother wrecked her car.

Julia and I used to take our dates there in later years when Aunt Julia and Uncle Sam lived out there. They would let us stay all night and we'd go hunting for duck on the lake, also doves in season, and quail; or to kill rattle snakes. That is where Percy convinced me he was the one for me, or was it vice versa? We all loved it out there.

Spence: Do you recall any interesting stories associated with Elmdale?

Jones: Oh, heavens, yes. There was a little country store about a half-mile from the ranch. The T&P train used to stop there if somebody flagged it down. One day after I had been hunting alone, except for my dog, Dan, I decided to go back to town on the train instead of having Uncle Sam drive me in. Dan was a cross between a collie and a German shepherd. He looked fierce. After a day hunting, I'm sure I looked fierce, too. Anyway, I flagged down the train, gun in hand and holding to Dan's collar. You wouldn't believe the looks I got from those passengers! The brakeman and I were good friends and we decided it might be better if we all stayed in the vestibule between cars and talked. Smart man.

Then there was quite a character running that little country store. He was a great friend of Judge's and in fact asked his advice on practically everything. One day he whispered to Judge that he had a particularly important question to ask. He took Judge to the back of the store, closed the door carefully, and continued whispering. He wanted some advice, he said, on a new investment he was thinking about. There had been a new oil strike near Elmdale and I am sure the storekeeper had had more business in a week than he had all the year before. He told Judge he was thinking about putting in a new line, and he wanted Judge's opinion: did Judge think he should put in a few five-cent cigars? Would they be likely to sell, or would he be stuck with them?

Judge never got tired of telling that story about high finance at Elmdale.

Spence: Can you describe the house at the Elmdale ranch?
Jones: Very primitive. Two bedrooms, a dining room, a large kitchen, a living room which was an extension of the kitchen, possibly, and a front porch across the entire house.
Spence: Judge Legett kept some of his cattle there at Elmdale?
Jones: Oh, yes.
Spence: Did he have a cattle brand?
Jones: Why, certainly.
Spence: Did Judge design it himself?
Jones: I don't remember, but I'm sure he did. I remember the brand, though. It was like this: KⒸ
Spence: How did he pronounce that?
Jones: You Easterners! Honey, that's Kay-Buckle. Now don't you ask me what Judge meant by that. I don't know.

Somehow this reminds me of one of my favorite stories about the family. It's also about the cattle buyers' market. Joe and Watt Matthews do business this way often. They know more or less what they are going to get for the cattle, but it is a gentlemen's agreement all the way.

One year the Matthews family shipped their calves per usual, seemingly up to their normal high standard, but before long the buyers wrote Joe or Watt and said the calves were showing a pronounced hump on their shoulders. You guessed it: some of the buffalo bulls had gotten in the wrong pasture. Would that make those calves "cattalo"? Joe and Watt were so embarrassed about it I doubt anyone would dare to try to tease them even now. You see, a cattleman's word of honor is something you don't toy with. Of course the shipment was made good and they all still do business with each other.

Spence: At what age did you most often go out to Elmdale?

Jones: That's hard to say. Maybe my late 'teens, when I discovered I could come and go as I pleased—within limits.

Spence: What were your other pastimes at about age eighteen?

Jones: Trying to make out I didn't care if no boy paid any mind to me. I was roughly one-half head taller than any boy that was anywhere near by age, so my only defense was to be rude to him. I was pretty successful. Julia was a natural and had loads of boyfriends. I was so embarrassed at being so tall I always claimed I didn't like to dance, but I was just dying to all the time. My personal opinion is I was quite messed up at that age.

Spence: Let's go to school for awhile: As a high school student, what subjects did you enjoy most?

Jones: History, always. In college I also enjoyed psychology, philosophy, and English literature. I flunked solid geometry twice. Had to memorize the book to ever pass it. Just a pretty average dumb sort of student. I was much more interested at school in sports such as basketball, tennis, swimming. Loved baseball whenever the boys would allow me to play, which wasn't often. Usually all they'd allow was for me to chase fly balls somewhere in the next county.

Spence: You are either exaggerating about solid geometry, or thinking about high school. I already know that you finished four years of college in three years for the bachelor's degree. You couldn't have done that if you had flunked any course.

Jones: Yes, it was in high school. I had sense enough to dodge solid geometry after that.

Spence: At Abilene High School you were the first editor of the school yearbook. This would indicate that, as a student, you were both intelligent and dependable.

Jones: Not necessarily. Miss Tommie Clack managed to get me involved in that job somehow. I was particularly dumb in English composition; used to get every theme paper marked on return: "Thought good, style rotten."

Spence: You are exaggerating again.

Jones: No, I am not. Really. I was a pretty sorry editor, I can assure you. I guess that nobody else would take the job. To this day I remember spelling door knob as door nob in an editorial. End of argument.

Spence: Were you the type of school child who would volunteer to do the difficult, boring jobs if nobody else would do them?

Jones: No! I said I was *average dumb.* Not *stupid.*

Spence: Shifting to another subject: Do you recall your father's involvement, while you were a 'teen-ager, in Abilene's effort to have Texas Tech located here?

Jones: Yes, indeed, but I was actually in my early twenties then. They were not calling it Texas Tech in those days. Seems it was West Texas A&M or something like that.

Spence: Do you recall that Abilene was first named as the winning site by the Location Committee appointed by the governor?

Jones: How could anyone in Abilene forget? And it was done fair and square Judge always said, although some things *looked* kind of shady.

Spence: Judge didn't believe that charge that Governor James E. Ferguson had deliberately miscounted the committee's vote?

Jones: Never. Not Judge.

Spence: Tell me all you remember about the case.

Jones: I may have half of it wrong, but here's how I recall how it concerned Judge. You must remember that there were other Abilene versions which make the Governor look guilty of charges against him. Judge just didn't believe them.

Well, at first the whole thing didn't mean too much to me, but Judge worked so hard, for so many weeks, getting up money, getting the right pieces of land put together for the campus, and so on, that I got interested. Everybody in Abilene did. Then, it seems, everybody in the state did. When Abilene finally lost, I can see Judge now, sitting at home with his head in his hands, the disappointment written all over him. He'd say he was such a dope for believing that Abilene or Central Texas could get that school when so many of the committee members had affiliations in Lubbock—or close to that part of the country. He'd then go over the committee names man by man and name how he thought each had voted.

I clearly remember when the committee was in Abilene. They went out to the house on Meander Street with Judge and looked out over the area south of town where the campus was supposed to be. I remember being on the porch when they came out of the house and stood there and talked. I think Judge really believed that somehow Abilene had been double-crossed.

Spence: Did you think that Abilene had been double-crossed?

Jones: I did at that time, but there were so many rumors, so many conflicting stories, that I don't know what I believe now.

Spence: What other interpretations of what happened can you recall?

Jones: I'm not sure I can put the pieces together . . . It seems that J.F. Cunningham [an Abilene attorney] was a very close friend of Governor Ferguson, and he spent the entire day, while the committee was here, at the Governor's elbow talking a-mile-a-minute.

All the members of the committee, you must remember, had sworn not to do any talking or to discuss the various locations until this secret ballot was taken, back in Austin. But on the way back to Austin, so the story went, Governor Ferguson comes back in the train, sits by President [W.B.] Bizzell of Texas A&M—who was not on the committee but was a consultant—and asks President Bizzell if he would help influence the committee's vote for Abilene. Jim Ferguson insisting that was the only place for it. This, remember, after several hours of constant talk with J.F. Cunningham.

When the committee finally met, each man wrote his selection—secretly—on a piece of paper and handed it to the Governor. The Governor looks at them each one, then announces that Abilene has received the most votes. Three out of five. Nobody asked to see the ballots, and they were destroyed. Later, some of the members got to talking and one said, "I didn't vote for Abilene." Then another said, "I didn't either." A third man said the same thing.

Well, you can imagine the uproar, but Jim Ferguson wouldn't reconvene the committee. Some time after that the Governor was impeached. For other reasons than this of course, but the legislature went and rescinded the bill. Much later, Texas Tech was placed at Lubbock.

Spence: And that's the end of the story?
Jones: Well, another version was that there was skulduggery, all right, but it didn't come from Jim Ferguson. Bob [Robert M.] Wagstaff told me just before he died that President Bizzell firmly held to this view: that somebody, but not the Governor, double-crossed the committee. The plot thickens every year and there are people living to this day that can get het-up over it. Teacher says that Dr. Ralph Steen of East Texas State University is the authority on Jim Ferguson.
Spence: Our time has run out again, and you have another appointment coming up.
Jones: I thought when I got this far along in life I'd be sitting in an easy chair taking life easy, and not even having to fan myself or pick up my own martini glass—but alas, 'tain't so!
Spence: Can you see Ruth Jones in an easy chair doing nothing?
Jones: No, honey. Never.

* * *

Spence: Good morning. Have you spent the last few weeks in your rockingchair having somebody to fan you while you doze off?
Jones: No! Old age, a small amount of brain power, and a ridiculous schedule are keeping the poor old mind in a state of

perpetual shock. Wouldn't you think that *nothing* could shock me at age eight-four?

Add to that an overnight trip to Texas A&M, my first trip down there ever—350 miles down and 350 miles back—and you can see why I may never remember anything else in my life.

But our A&M trip was fun. Teacher, Dr. Aston, Dorothy Stowe, and I drove down. There were two parties going at once: it being Buck Schiewitz's birthday party and an autograph party for a beautiful new book on Texas. There were five hundred people at the Chancellor's house for the first party and about two hundred at the party that night. I was dead, no nap, no place to sit down, and barbecue—not my dish—upstairs, but no elevator to get to the dining room. I stayed at each party about thirty minutes and then had to go back to the hotel. I did enjoy it all, though, and *must* have met some very important people. Teacher will explain to me later who they are. I did run into my favorite cousin, my only one really. I didn't know he would be there. That's Texas Trammell.

Spence: Didn't you recognize anyone else?

Jones: Well, I saw that Professor you-know-who. He wasn't rude or even impolite, but he just looked a little ill at ease, and like he wished he could think of something polite and diplomatic to say. I believe that poor man has less spark, less smile, less joy of life about him than anybody I ever saw. I felt like when I had made a remark that I had written it on a piece of paper and thrown it in the trash basket. I asked Teacher if he thought I had said something wrong and he said he didn't know. Surely I am not that blah.

Oh, I saw Ann Brindley, who wrote that nice note to me after *Judge Legett of Abilene* came out. She has been past president of the Texas State Historical Association. I have always liked her.

But, guess what? Mr. Wardlaw called me right back not long after I was down at A&M and asked us to another party in Austin in March. Ain't that something? He said he was having a few writers, authors, and so on, at the Villa Capri one night before the TSHA meeting begins. He asked in particular if you were coming down for the meeting, so he could invite you and Wanda. I told him I sure hope you do. Why don't you?

Spence: Sounds like a lot of fun, but since I have no part on the program we probably won't come back for that meeting. The University pays my expenses only if I participate. You and Teacher have fun and tell me about it next time we get together. Right now I have some questions for you.

Jones: Fire away.

Spence: First, about Kade and Julia: Did they ever finish college?

Jones: They didn't either one finish. Julia didn't like Ward-Belmont, so Judge let her go on a several months' tour of Europe. When she returned she came by Randolph-Macon to see me. She showed up at my dormitory with one steamer trunk that had one Paris gown, two slippers that didn't match and not much of anything else. Later on she went to the University of Texas and did very well, but she didn't finish.

I stayed at Randolph-Macon for two years and then came home and finished at Simmons. I wasn't so interested either, but Mother and Judge seemed so disappointed that not one of their young'uns had gotten a degree, so I bowed my neck and went back—went out to Simmons every morning on the street car. Judge seemed to appreciate it.

Kade had gone off to Vanderbilt to school. Not for long, because his mind was definitely not on school. Julia was in Nashville at Ward-Belmont that same year. Judge and Mother wanted her far enough away from Abilene to get over a crush on the laundry delivery boy.

Well, as you can plainly see, *I* was the only completely perfect child Judge and Mother had. Reckon?

Spence: No comment. Let me go back to an earlier conversation we've had: You mentioned breaking your collar bone by falling, or being pushed, off a donkey on your way to school with Julia and Kade . . .

Jones: Yes.

Spence: . . . but I thought earlier you said it was your shoulder?

Jones: That, too! But I was at the University of Texas taking

graduate courses when I broke my shoulder. That was the year after I finished at Simmons.
Spence: Well, tell me about it. Did the horse throw you?
Jones: He most certainly did *not* throw me! He fell! It was my right shoulder, but before I tell you about it, let me mention a side story: I had called the livery stable from my room. I told them to send me a *good* horse, otherwise I knew, because I was a woman, that they would send me an old plug to ride. I had to insist that I was an accomplished rider, that I could ride anything.

Now, back to the beginning: the horse stumbled on a street car track near the University and I hit on my right shoulder. I picked myself up, got back on the horse—don't ask me how—and rode him back to the infirmary, and there they taped my shoulder. Then, I had to call the livery stable to come get the horse. I don't know the horse's name. I nearly went through the floor when they asked me where the horse was—in front of the infirmary! I could just hear them snickering, "Isn't that just like a woman? She said she would ride anything."

Well, I was already in love with Percy and I guess I used that injury as an excuse to come home before the mid-term exams.
Spence: What would you say if I suggested that you were still competing with your brother, Kade, when you insisted on their sending you a "good" horse?
Jones: I'd say you are probably right. I guess that's why I was skinning my knee or breaking my bones so much. Just like him. But, oh my, Kade was the original accident kid. I hardly got hurt at all compared to him. But we've already talked about that.
Spence: Let's talk instead about your marriage to Percy. You and Julia both married in 1915—Julia to Dr. Luther James Pickard in February, and you to Percy Jones, a young Welsh civil engineer who had joined his uncle, Morgan Jones, in railroading, in December.
Jones: Yes. We thought Judge would die—losing both of his daughters in the same year—but he survived nicely.

Spence: And you really did catch the bride's bouquet at Julia's wedding?

Jones: Just goes to show that some myths have some basis in fact. But I caught more than Julia's bouquet; I think I still have cedar needles in my hands from decorating the old Baptist church. No catering, no contracting services in those days. Like so many other things, you either did it yourself or it didn't get done.

Fay Morton and I had charge of the wedding. I guess today that would make us mistresses of ceremonies? I don't remember why, but it seems like nobody else in the family gave us the slightest bit of help. Also, we gave a huge house party, made all the blind dates for the girls in the wedding and house party, washed dishes. Everything. It wouldn't surprise me if the records show that Fay and I went out and bought the marriage license.

Spence: You and Percy had a much shorter engagement and a simpler wedding than Julia.

Jones: You bet. I couldn't go through all of that again in the same year.

Spence: Why?

Jones: Oh, my, you historians can get nosey! I thought I just told you: I still had cedar needles in my hands from Julia's wedding.

Spence: Not much of an answer.

Jones: Well, number one: I was afraid Percy would get away. If that doesn't satisfy you: The Old Mahn might send him to Timbuktu or Topolobampo to build another railroad. Or number three: Maybe he'd go back to Wales.

But would you believe the Old Mahn got into our act after all! As we left on our honeymoon he told Percy to go by Lampasas to take care of some business! Percy at least waited until we were on our way home again before we headed for Lampasas. Then—and this is the truth—Percy says after we get there that the business will take him a couple of days, so why don't I go back to Abilene ahead of him! I told him I'd die first. Imagine me coming home from my honeymoon *alone!*

Spence: A great story. Now tell me more about Percy.
Jones: He had a sweet smile, placid disposition, an understanding nature, and he was the epitome of reasonableness. A grand guy in anybody's book.
Spence: Do you remember when you were first introduced to him?
Jones: No, but I had seen Percy at parties a time or two before we ever met.
Spence: Do you remember your first date?
Jones: Indeed I do. He called on the telephone for a date. I was especially pleased because as far as I knew he hadn't been with any Abilene girl. Of course an unmarried eligible man was great news, and much gossip drifted about town before anybody really knew him. We went out on our date and had a very nice time. And then I never let him get away.

Now I'll confess something: I didn't know for years that when he called our house he *thought* he was talking to Julia when he asked for a date. He didn't know his mistake until he came to the house and I came out. He sure didn't bat an eyelash. Just goes to show that one can never tell what fate has in store. My good luck.
Spence: Tell me about your courtship.
Jones: Our *favorite* dates were spent riding on the railroad hand-car . . . Fooled you didn't I? Percy would have someone place the hand-car on the Abilene and Southern tracks after all the trains had come in for the night. There was just enough chance of its jumping the track to make it fun. Percy looked quite glamorous to me as he wheeled us away from town through the darkness. There wasn't much chance for hanky-panky to be sure.

One night we came near to having a very serious accident. We were tooting along at about thirty miles an hour, me with my feet hung over the side of the little car and *wham!,* barbed wire was wrapping all around us. You see, the farmers along the right-of-way had, earlier that day, strung bob-wire along the tracks and pastured their cattle right up to the rails, where the grass was usually very green. The farmers knew they could move the fence back before the trains came along next morning.

The only thing that kept me from having two stumps instead of two feet is that I was wearing high-button buckskin shoes. They were cut to ribbons. When Percy saw blood on the shoes he made me show him where my legs were cut. I was mortified; he had to marry me after that. You must remember those were the days when Queen Victoria's ideas ruled the roost.

Spence: Do you have any other stories about Percy that you would like to share?

Jones: Let me think . . . These two stories go under household sayings in the Jones family, and they involve Percy: He had a delightful broad a when he first came to this country but gradually lost it, for he was teased about it all the time. He wanted to lose it because it made him different. I tried to talk him out of working to lose it, but no good.

Well, just before we got married, he and C.G. Whitten were quite good friends, and C.G. made Percy promise he would tell him the real truth about marriage after he had been married two or three weeks. And *nothing but the truth.* The time came when Percy could put him off no longer, so he drew a deep breath and unconsciously slipped into his broad a: "Well," he says, "I'll tell you, Whit, it has its advantages and its disadvantages."

We never let Percy forget that. Every evaluation we ever made from then on out was described in just that way. Then, at another time, I asked Percy one day—silly woman—if he would ever marry again if I died before he did. He quickly and seriously said, "Hell, no! Once is enough!" And that's what I got for sticking my neck out.

Spence: Yes. Served you right . . . and that's a good closing note for today . . . have you been behaving yourself lately?

Jones: How lately?

Spence: Well, let's say since our last meeting.

Jones: Indeed I have. I gave almost all of our pictures of the Abilene and Southern Railroad to Everett DeGolyer of Dallas. I didn't have many to give, but he has a fabulous collection of railroad pictures. The one I like best from the Abilene and

Southern was of a high bridge at Seymour which Percy always said he built with a screwdriver and a block-and-tackle. DeGolyer is an oilman, art collector, patron of Southern Methodist University, you name it. Percy once had him to help assess the value of some oil property of ours. A famous geologist, too. He developed some "new geology" or something.

But it's really been too hot for *anybody* to misbehave. I feel very imposed upon, and the whole state of Texas seems to be in bad humor. I've had a bunch of silly, unnecessary things to happen since our last meeting: a broken toe the last one. But enough of me. I'm sick of me.

And then, a big inconvenience has overtaken Teacher and me. We are both getting to where we can't see very well to drive at night, and he won't hear of anybody driving for us. Students by the droves are available, but I suspect Teacher feels like he'd be slipping if he gives up doing anything he could do fifty years ago. He has recently had a peculiar illness, something the matter with his innards, but Dr. Webster can't find anything. They have each promised the other that, if the party of the first part finds out what it is, he will report it to the part of the second part.

Teacher always gets to my house before dark. Somehow he feels he will be perfectly safe driving *from* my house to his house, no matter what time of night or how dark.

* * *

Jones: Good morning. Are we all in our places with sunshiny faces? It seems like old times to get together. I enjoy it immensely.
Spence: Good morning. It's been so long, maybe you had better give an account of yourself.
Jones: You never let me have *any* secrets. Maybe I've been out racing trains. To tell the truth, I've been working pretty diligently for a month or more moving out furniture from my Dallas apartment to a suite here in the new retirement home at Hendrick Hospital that Boone Powell so kindly let me and my

family have . . . forever, I guess. Sounds like a good idea to me. I have always had a horror of becoming dependent on my young'uns when I cannot take care of myself and couldn't get any help. Edith [her daughter, Edith O'Donnell] checked out the apartment, and Judy [her daughter, Julia Matthews] and I worked this end of it. I had no idea it would be such a job. The Home is nearly through now. Just hope the whole idea will benefit some old folks who don't have anybody to take care of them. I hope I don't have to move there right away, but meanwhile it is a nice place to stay when I'm under the weather.

And would you believe I'm actually going to fly again? I'm going to Houston in November to a board meeting at the M.D. Anderson Hospital. Ain't that something? I have no idea I'll live through the ordeal, but have given my word to Judy. She will be going with me.

Spence: Congratulations for all sorts of things you have just told me, but especially for one that you haven't mentioned: your new doctorate from McMurry College.

Jones: Isn't that too much!

Spence: No, it isn't. I support entirely the comments in a recent *Abilene Reporter-News* editorial . . .

Jones: Now you know I'm easily embarrassed and I don't like my face to turn red, so let's get on with our work.

Spence: All right, Dr. Jones, you just brought up the subject of airplanes, so here's a question about them: You were with Percy when you took your first airplane ride, weren't you?

Jones: Well, yes and no. My first ride was from California to Kansas City. I had taken Buddy [her only son, Grenville Dodge Jones, who died as a youth] to a special school in California. The Adams School, I believe it was. Percy wrote from Abilene and said he was going to New York on business and suggested I meet him at Kansas City. So off I went. Got a thrill the first time I flew over the Mississippi River, but couldn't stand flying. Never liked the blasted things. Too wobbly. Never have flown unless I had to and not at all in recent years. Always preferred to drive or make a reservation by Pullman. But this time I've promised Judy.

Spence: Let me move forward to World War II for just one question. I found some newspaper items and wonder if you can add any information about the work you did on the home front during the second war?
Jones: Not really. Quite routine, except for making that Red Cross office from an old chicken coop. I visited just about every little town in this area seeking and *getting* a lot of help and supplies for "Bundles for Britain" and "British War Relief." We sent gobs of materials and quite a bit of money, quilts, and so on. I remember a rancher and his wife—their ranch was between Eden and San Angelo—who were especially helpful. Haven't seen them since, and I don't remember their names.
Spence: Fine. Now let's go back to the thirties and the Great Depression. Were the Joneses particularly affected by the Great Depression?
Jones: I can't remember too much personal privation for us. Those were also the days when we were so distressed over Buddy's health that nothing else seemed to matter. I guess the way the Depression affected me most, though, was that I became much more compassionate toward beggars at our back door. We had never seen very much of that before.
Spence: Did you join the Episcopal church when you married Percy Jones?
Jones: No, quite a few years later. My joining the Episcopal church was a little unusual. You see, Percy's and my whole lives were changed by our dear Buddy's illness. Percy was born into the Church of England, but had not affiliated himself with any church in this country. When the children were small, Percy decided he would join the Episcopal church. When Percy and the children were ready—after much instruction—Parson [Willis P.] Gerhart gave them a private Sunday afternoon session, while the Bishop was here.

    I sat back in the last pew to watch, but when I saw all that cute tribe of mine going up there I couldn't stand it. I pulled off my hat and walked up there just after they had all stepped to the altar. Nobody knew I was going to do it, especially me—bless Parson and all—nobody batted an eye. Everything went off as if it had been planned for weeks until I looked around and saw Edith slipping quietly to the floor. Not a sound, not a mutter. She just folded up. I'm not sure, but I think some of the holy water was used for other purposes and she came to in a few minutes and with the sweetest smile you ever saw on a human face.

Everybody had been so watchful and apprehensive about Buddy we hadn't even thought about Edith and Julia. There were only a few others in the church, but Erle Sellers, our doctor, was there. Edith has been teased all her life about how hard religion comes to some people.

Spence: Let's assume that all mothers love their daughters, so we can move on to the subject of friendship: Was there an obvious camaraderie between Sophia and her daughters, and Lora and her daughters, as there is between you and your daughters?

Jones: There aren't anywhere any such relationships. I could go on, but do I need to? They are fine, beautiful, loyal, understanding, Christian, and, above all, wonderful daughters.

Spence: We have seen that Sophia's daughter, and Lora's daughter, and Ruth's two daughters went to schools in Virginia. Was this a coincidence or was it deliberate?

Jones: More a coincidence. Lora went to Virginia because Sophia's people were from up that way. I've always thought, too, that the Bryans' close friendship with Congressman Roger Q. Mills had something to do with it. You know, I can't remember why I went to Randolph-Macon Women's College. Maybe Mother influenced me; she always wanted us to "see the world." We let Judy pick Madeira in Virginia because a friend of hers from Fort Worth wanted to go there and the friend had an aunt living nearby in Washington. Edith went there because Judy did.

Spence: Tell me again about your packing a gun to take with you to Randolph-Macon.

Jones: It is true, but after all, I left the clip out when I carried the gun in my purse which, as far as I was concerned, made it perfectly safe. I wouldn't have thought of going off into a strange country without my gun.

Spence: But you knew better than to tell Judge or your mother.
Jones: I was a 'teen-ager, so naturally it wasn't any of their business. Now wouldn't I die if one of my children or grandchildren had done a thing like that?
Spence: Apparently, those family trips during your childhood influenced the great distances all of you traveled to college.
Jones: I was born loving to travel, and Mother's love of it, I am sure, only augmented it. After Percy's death, sister Julia and I almost lived on ships for several years. I can't think of many run-of-the-mill places I haven't been many times over: England, Wales, Scotland, Norway, Sweden—all over Europe; North Africa—and all around Africa and on a special train from Cape Town to Johannesburg; India, Hawaii lots of times; all over South America; all over Mexico; Canada—east, west and all over; Alaska; all over the Caribbean several times; the Philippines; Borneo, Java . . . Now aren't you sorry you asked?
Spence: No. I knew you had traveled, but not so extensively. Here's another spot question: If you were writing a Ruth Legett Jones autobiography, what confessions would you make?
Jones: Now this reminds me of those stories of prisoners having to dig their own graves and then standing on the edge and getting shot. I thought I had already confessed every thought, every recollection, every move I ever made.
Spence: I thought I might get some sort of self-image from you.
Jones: Well, I guess I never got credit or blame for what I was: that is, a natural bit of a hussy. It's just as well, I guess, because it would have put Mother and Judge in their early graves.

You see, as I said before, Julia was pretty and cute and all the boys naturally loved her. I tried to be like her, but it didn't work one bit. So I just had to wait until after eighty to knock 'em dead—and that's not easy!

I wish I knew what makes me bare *all* to you. Things I have never told anybody. Maybe I feel like I'll be "daid" before any of this comes out.
Spence: I'm pretty sure the readers will recognize a natural tease when they read about one. You're not fooling anybody, especially me. Let me ask you one more comparison-question:

Do you think it would be accurate to say that Sophia Bryan, Lora Legett, and Ruth Jones were not the "clinging vine" type as wives?
Jones: You bet it would be accurate. Can't imagine either of us as clinging vine.
Spence: You were not, or did not feel like, mere shadows of your husbands?
Jones: No, not even Granny Bryan way back in those days. We were all proud of our husbands and wanted to see them succeed. But instead of clinging vines, or trailing along behind them, we were more likely nudging them along and trying to help.
Spence: All three of you were able and willing to act independently when the occasions arose.
Jones: Yes, and there were times when we had opportunities to prove it.
Spence: Were any of you the superstitious type? Did you believe in old wives' tales, or that sort of thing?
Jones: I'm glad you brought that up; I would have forgotten to mention it. The answer is No! with a capital N. All three of us couldn't abide superstitions or superstitious people. Ignorance breeds superstition. All of us were too practical, or too realistic, or too busy, I guess, to sit around and imagine such fantasies.
Spence: Let's go back again to Abilene's early history: Do you recall talking to Judge about the first day of Abilene's existence, or the day the first town-lot auction was held?
Jones: Very little. To tell the truth I had forgot that Judge was there that day until you dug it up for *Judge Legett of Abilene*.

There were so many "firsts" in his life he just didn't appreciate its historical importance. But I can tell you something about that vacant lot—well, they were all vacant that day, weren't they?—where the auction was held. It was at South First and Chestnut, the very same corner where Police Chief [John J.] Clinton stood every New Year's Eve night, for many years, to welcome in the new year. It got to be a tradition and crowds gathered there with him every year. Anyway, we owned that lot for a long time. I gave it to the city a few years back. Highways and city planning had cut into it so much it really wasn't worth much any more.

But the lot also had the old Abney Building on it. I'm quite sure the Old Mahn named the building after one of his friends. One of the oldest, if not the oldest and only, Opera House in town was located in the Abney Building. I hate to admit I had it torn down some years ago. I had it razed for fear a high West Texas wind would blow it down some fine March day. My agent tried to tell me it was still strong, but a building in Dallas had collapsed a few weeks before, killing several people, so the old Abney Building hit the dust. 'Twould be a nice corner for a historical marker some day, wouldn't it?

Neal Hollingshead had a very ambitious undertaking a year or so ago for that corner. He wanted to take the entire block and call it Clinton Square. He was going to spend umpteen dollars on it and reproduce as near as possible a replica of what it was in those early days. Judge had an office over a saloon just across on the west side of South First and Chestnut. Somehow, Neal's whole plan fell through—couldn't get any encouragement from Austin, or something like that. Too bad; it was a wonderful idea.

Spence: Very little has been written about women in Abilene's history. There are a few outstanding exceptions, such as Mary Hampton Clack's *Early Days in West Texas* and Katharyn Duff's, Tommie Clack's and Betty Kay Seibt's *Pioneer Days . . . Two Views.* Would you name some of the Abilene women who, in your opinion, should be researched and written about?

Jones: Oh, so many; some of them with fascinating stories to tell of their own experiences: the Clack sisters, the Fletcher girls, Mrs. Sears who raised six or eight young'uns, all girls but one, by herself on a ranch, with Indians all over the place; Mrs. Dallas Scarborough; Mrs. Hill, who drove through the country by herself with a wagon full of young children, and Indians all along the way; Mrs. J.M. Radford. Dozens of others whose stories should be told.

Spence: You realize, don't you, that some day we're going to have to make a complete list of your philanthropies and gifts to charity?

Jones: I declare, Vernon, what do you want to do, take all the fun out of so-called charitable work? Now you be quiet . . . you are not serious, are you?

Spence: We're going to be leaving out a big part of your story if we don't tell about the little long-legged, self-conscious pioneer girl who grew up to be one of the leading philanthropists in Texas.

Jones: I'd rather just lump it all together and put it in one paragraph someplace, with no footnotes.

Spence: You have just sent a large check to renovate Legett Hall at Texas A&M, and you want to "lump" that in with the smaller gifts to send young men and women off to college, and so forth?

Jones: I'd rather be a part of the stories written about those I've helped.

Spence: You have done some *noble* things with your wealth, Mrs. Jones; there's no harm in making it a part of Abilene's history.

Jones: I hope I live long enough to do something noble somewhere for somebody. I am afraid that old calendar will get me before I can do half I want to.

Spence: You'll live to see your great-great-grandchildren, and then some. Our time is up again.

Jones: Now don't tell me to behave. Judy and John are in Paris for awhile and I can do what I want to.

You are always asking me questions, let me ask you one. In fact I've been remiss in not asking before: How is Kevin enjoying studying architecture in Switzerland?

Spence: He thinks he's died and gone to heaven.

Jones: I am so used up after our conversations I haven't thought of anything nice enough to say about him. Tell him I'm proud of him, and slip in a nice grandmotherly kiss when you see him in London at Christmas.

Spence: I'll do that; and he'll be flattered.

Jones: And tell him I said go ahead, tear down an Alp or two, build a castle or two in its place.

* * *

EPILOGUE

Ruth Legett Jones died suddenly at her home in Abilene on October 14, 1978. She was eighty-five years old and, at the time of her death, her life spanned all but the first decade of Abilene's existence.

A banner headline on the front page of the *Abilene Reporter-News* informed its readers that the city had lost its "quiet philanthropist." An editorial in the same newspaper emphasized the significant role she and her family had played throughout Abilene's ninety-seven-year history. The editor noted her genuine interest in history, and especially in West Texas history, and concluded that "Abilene is a far better place for her having been a part of it so long."

Eulogies from friends and beneficiaries throughout the Southwest praised the "lady of grace, gentility, high intelligence, wit, and good humor." They noted the glee with which she sometimes gave away her money, and her constant insistence that she gained far more from her gifts than those who received them. She insisted also that few of those whom she tried to help had disappointed her.

Ruth Jones would have been pleased, but genuinely surprised, to know that Texas Governor Bill Clements attended her funeral service at the Episcopal Church of the Heavenly Rest in Abilene. The church itself stands on the same city lot on Meander Street where her father had built the Legett mansion. It is a fitting reminder of the generosity which she practiced as if it were a religion.

Her long-time friend, historian Rupert Norval Richardson, solaced a bereaved West Texas city with the reminder that Ruth Legett Jones was allotted a relatively long span of years and that "she lived in full measure just about every one of them."

BIBLIOGRAPHICAL NOTE

It should come as no great surprise that my primary sources for this book, both written and oral, are almost exclusively located in Abilene, Texas. Nevertheless, my shirt sleeves have dusted table tops in such scattered places as the Denver (Colorado) Public Library; the University archives at Texas A&M; the Federal Archives and Records Center, General Services Administration, Fort Worth; and the National Archives and Library of Congress just across the Potomac River from my home in Virginia.

Since 1967 I have centered most of my research in such locally rich repositories as the morgue at the *Abilene Reporter-News,* the libraries at McMurry College, Abilene Christian University, and Hardin-Simmons University (including the Richardson Research Center), the Abilene Public Library, the Taylor County Court House, and the offices of the Percy Jones Estate located in the First National-Ely Building in Abilene. The Morgan Jones papers have since been moved from the First National-Ely Building to Texas Tech University in Lubbock, and the K.K. Legett papers are now at the Richardson Research Center at Hardin-Simmons University.

Family business records and genealogical papers were invaluable to the preparation of this book. Nevertheless, until Ruth Legett Jones came along, the Bryans, Legetts, and Joneses—a busy lot—were not given to leaving unbroken lines for future historians. I have found it necessary, therefore, to search for them in every existent issue of the *Abilene Reporter* the *Abilene Daily Reporter,* the *Abilene Weekly Reporter,* the *Abilene Morning Reporter,* the *Buffalo Gap News,* and the *Taylor County News* between the years 1880 and 1926—not once but twice. The only trauma along the way occurred when I discovered that not a single Abilene or Taylor County newspaper exists for the years 1901-02-03. (No, I do not have an explanation.)

Several other useful collections of West Texas family records and genealogies located in the Abilene libraries include the W.J. Bryan papers, the R.C. Crane papers, the Alfred E. Mann papers, and the Robert S. Simmons papers. Helpful unpublished theses at Hardin-Simmons University include Naomi Hatton Kincaid, "The *Abilene Reporter-News* and its Contributions to the Development of the Abilene Country"; Emmett M. Landers, "A Short History of Taylor County"; Samuel Luther Robertson, Jr., "The Life Story of William John Bryan, 1859-1948"; and Irene Stewart, "James A. Lowery and the *Taylor County News.*"

The various Abilene repositories also hold virtually complete collections of the *West Texas Historical Association Year Book* and the *Southwestern Historical Quarterly*, two scholarly journals which are especially rich in West Texas history. Among the articles I found most useful from these two journals are Tommie Clack, "Buffalo Gap College" (*WTHAYB*); R.C. Crane, "The Beginning of Hardin-Simmons University," and "When West Texas Was in the Making" (*WTHAYB*); W.C. Holden, "Immigration and Settlement in West Texas" (*WTHAYB*); Naomi Kincaid, "The Founding of Abilene, the 'Future Great' of the Texas and Pacific Railway" (*WTHAYB*); J.W. Williams, "Robson's Journey Through West Texas in 1879," (*WTHAYB*); and Wayne Gard, "The Impact of the Cattle Trails" (*SHQ*). Such articles as Seymour V. Connor, "Early Land Speculation in West Texas" (*Southwestern Social Science Quarterly*) and Oliver Knight, "Toward an Understanding of the Western Town" (*Western Historical Quarterly*), proved equally useful.

Books on Abilene and the Big Country area—many of them written by West Texans—are becoming increasingly plentiful (although many more are needed) and they provided a valuable historical context for this book. Among them are Rupert Norval Richardson, *Famous Are Thy Halls: Hardin-Simmons University as I Have Known It (1964);* T.S. Rollins, *Taylor County: An Early History of Pioneer Settlers (1923);* Zane Allen Mason, *Frontiersmen of the Faith: A History of Bap-*

tist Pioneer Work in Texas, 1865-1885 (1970); Katharyn Duff, *Abilene . . . On Catclaw Creek: A Profile of a West Texas Town* (1969), and, with Tommie Clack and Betty Kay Seibt, *Pioneer Days . . . Two Views* (1979); Hugh E. Cosby (ed.), *History of Abilene* (1955); and Mary Hampton Clack, *Early Days in West Texas* (1932). My earlier books: *Colonel Morgan Jones: Grand Old Man of Texas Railroading* (1971) and *Judge Legett of Abilene: A Texas Frontier Profile* (1977) provide a more immediate family history context for the subject of this book.

Having mentioned a representative collection of written sources upon which I depended, I hasten to emphasize my greater dependence upon the oral sources. My debt to the late Ruth Legett Jones is obvious to anyone who reads this book. For twelve years we talked . . . and talked. Sometimes she reminisced for an hour or more by telephone between Texas and Virginia. On other occasions we talked in her Abilene office or in her home. Only my firm promise to her prevents my sharing authorship with her. I made one other promise to Mrs. Jones concerning the preparation of this book, and it turned out to be the only attempt she ever made to influence my writing or my methods. It concerned the use of footnotes. She could not abide them and no one, not even Rupert Richardson, could convince her that the reading public wants them. I kept my promise by designing a format which, I hope, makes footnotes generally unnecessary.

Others with whom I conducted interviews for this and my previous books (beginning back in 1967) include Miss Bobbie Clack, Miss Tommie Clack, Katharyn Duff, Ruth Bradfield Gay, Julia Legett Pickard, Willis P. Gerhart, Walter S. Pope, W.G. Swenson, C.L. Hailey, and Rupert N. Richardson.